Spoiling Python's Schemes

Spoiling Python's Schemes

Bobbie Jean Merck

A Great Love, Inc.
Toccoa, Georgia

Unless otherwise indicated, all scriptural quotations are from the *King James Version* of the Bible.

Spoiling Python's Schemes
ISBN 0-929263-02-2
Copyright © 1990 by
A Great Love, Inc.
P.O. Box 1248
Toccoa, GA 30577

Second Printing, August 1993

Published by
A Great Love, Inc.
P.O. Box 1248
Toccoa, GA 30577
U.S.A.

Cover design and book production by
DB & Associates Design Group, Inc.
P.O. Box 52756
Tulsa, OK 74152

Contents

Introduction

Whenever a book of this nature is being presented, there needs to be consideration given to purpose, intent, and sound biblical basis. In dealing with topics related to demonic activity, we have seen in the body of Christ, the full range from total denial to bizarre behavior. There is no doubt that the subject of demons causes controversy within the Christian community. However, to ignore the subject entirely would also be a mistake. We are instructed in 2 Corinthians 2:11, to be wise and not ignorant of Satan's devices.

In approaching this subject, it is my intent to remain fixed in the Word of God, because therein is security, stability, and truth. Because of its controversial nature, I have had to seriously weigh the decision to release this work. With much prayer and direction by the Lord, I am releasing it with the strong exhortation that it is for *information*, and not for *fascination*.

This information is *not* intended to be used as the basis of criticism or assessments about individuals. It is meant to expose the enemy, not condemn God's people. First Timothy 4:1-6 speaks of seducing spirits and the latter times, closing with, "If thou put the brethren in remembrance of these things, thou shalt be a good minister of Jesus Christ, nourished up in the words of faith and of good doctrine, whereunto thou hast attained."

In Ephesians 6:10-18, God specifically tells us that

our battles are not against flesh and blood, but rather, principalities and powers in the heavenlies. In Colossians 2:15, it is said of Jesus, "And having spoiled principalities and powers, he made a shew of them openly, triumphing over them in it." Because He is in us, and we have the power of the Holy Spirit, we have been given power and authority to do the same.

Ephesians 6:10 lets us know that it is through the power of our Lord Jesus, that we are able to stand against the plots and schemes of the enemy. According to Ephesians 6:13-17, we have His armor and sword of the Spirit available for our protection. We have no cause to fear the enemy or any knowledge about him. Isaiah 54:17 declares, "No weapon that is formed against thee shall prosper; and every tongue that shall rise against thee in judgment thou shalt condemn. This is the heritage of the servants of the Lord, and their righteousness is of me, saith the Lord."

Because of their frequently bizarre manifestations, some people have become fascinated with the operations of demons. However, because of the subtle devices of the adversary, we must not let ourselves be caught up in the snare of constantly thinking and talking about demons and their activities.

Instead, we should continuously be mindful of God and His Word. In so doing, we choose to meditate on the knowledge of life, which will bring us victorious living.

PHILIPPIANS 4:8

8 Finally, brethren, whatsoever things are true, whatsoever things are honest, whatsoever things are just, whatsoever things are pure, whatsoever things are lovely, whatsoever things are of good report; if there be any virtue, and if there be any praise, think on these things.

Let your conversation and meditation, therefore, be about God and that which is godly. Remember that He forbade Israel to put the name of another god in their mouth. Choose life! (Compare Deuteronomy 30:19,20.)

We are to expect and look for the very best in everyone. However, we are not to attribute everything that is contrary to the Word to be the work of demons, because most assuredly, flesh is involved.

Remember that as you perceive all people, expect the best of them as we are exhorted to do in 1 Corinthians 13:4-8. Verse 5 of 1 Corinthians 13, Ben Campbell Johnson paraphrase, states this principle in a most profound way. "Love is not rude or grasping or overly sensitive, nor does love search for imperfections and faults in others." Look for the best in people, yet do not be ignorant of Satan's devices.

Again, to emphasize the importance of my original statements, as you read these chapters, remember that they are for *information*, not *fascination*. They are *not* intended to arouse curiosity about demonic activity, but to simply expose the devices of the enemy so that God's people can walk in the liberty that Jesus Christ purchased for us.

We are to follow the full scope of the ministry of the Lord Jesus Christ. We are not to single out one aspect, and say, "I have a deliverance ministry." Rather, we need to understand that we have the ministry of the Lord Jesus Christ.

In this regard, we continuously need to be reminded to always guard our hearts. This calls for a balanced approach to the whole counsel of God, and a balanced walk in the fullness of ministry, which is abundantly evident in Luke 10:17-20.

LUKE 10:17-20

17 And the seventy returned again with joy, saying, Lord, even the devils are subject unto us through thy name.

18 And he said unto them, I beheld Satan as lightning fall from heaven.

19 Behold, I give unto you power to tread on serpents and scorpions, and over all the power of the enemy: and nothing shall by any means hurt you.

20 Notwithstanding in this rejoice not, that the spirits are subject unto you; but rather rejoice, because your names are written in heaven.

Herein, I believe is the scriptural safeguard. We should simply take authority over demons and cast them out. We do not need to become distracted or amused with them, and let them occupy time in our thought life or conversation. Rather, let us focus our attention on rejoicing that our names are written in heaven.

1 PETER 5:8

8 Be sober, be vigilant; because your adversary the devil, as a roaring lion, walketh about, seeking whom he may devour.

1 JOHN 3:8b

8 ...For this purpose the Son of God was manifested, that he might destroy the works of the devil.

Remember also that Jesus said, "...as my Father hath sent me, even so send I you" (John 20:21b).

Followers of Jesus Christ have been called by God to be as Jesus in this earth, that we might have victory in reality over the works of the devil through the power of the Name of the Lord Jesus Christ, and the power of the Holy Spirit. Our confidence is in the knowledge that we are purchased by and covered with the blood of Jesus Christ, our Lord and Savior. May this book serve in advancing the kingdom of God in this earth through you, the reader, that you become exercised in the power of the Holy Spirit to the pulling down of strongholds over all that concerns you. Be blessed in the precious Name of Jesus.

Spoiling Python's Schemes

Chapter 1
Python In Action

There have been countless people who have truly heard from God to do a mighty work in a particular location. They are obedient in starting a church, and it begins to grow, moving forward into accomplishing the vision for that local body. They reach membership of perhaps seventy-five or one hundred, when seemingly the powers of darkness break loose with their fruit of division, strife, jealousy, and every evil thing. The work falls apart, and needs to be built up all over again.

This sad scenario is even more frustrating in that the pattern is cyclical, and so we find the process is repeated again and again. With each turn of the cycle there is more discouragement, frustration, and weariness. Questions begin, who is right or wrong, even questions concerning the call and gifts.

When people wander from church to church, not becoming rooted and established in a local body, it is a part of the same issue. Just when they reach a place of alignment and being grounded in the church, they hit an impenetrable wall. It's like a brazen sky, and the breakthrough they need is denied them. So they pick up and search for a new place in hope of finding the elusive factor that would give them peace.

The problem cannot be fully attributed to the pastor, the leaders, or the sheep. We must understand that the

1

problem is not flesh and blood, even though it works through human beings. The thief is working against whoever he can to steal, kill, and destroy.

As you relate to these "war stories", you will begin to see how evil beings have operated against you in your own life, home, and church. The underlying principle is, that unless you deal with the ruling prince, you will not have a continuous breakthrough. You will experience a momentary release from the opposition that is operating against you, but just when you think you have the victory, its ugly head will raise up again.

The world system offers a generous array of alternatives, programs, movements, and religions motivated by the spirit of divination, otherwise known as the spirit of python. They offer notions about the spirit world that date back to the beginning of man, devoid of the knowledge of God. They are colorfully packaged in ritual and tradition, but all end up with the same cruel bottom line.

One such movement currently in vogue is the "New Age" movement, which is about as new as ancient Babylon, having the same ruling spirit that controlled Nimrod. None of these religions offer a Savior like Jesus, who saves to the uttermost and gives us power for living now and eternally.

Jesus Cast Out Demons

We must first understand that demons are very real disembodied spirits, who move about on the earth. Jesus spoke of this in Matthew 12:43-45.

MATTHEW 12:43-45

43 When the unclean spirit is gone out of a man, he walketh through dry places, seeking rest, and findeth none.

44 Then he saith, I will return into my house from whence I came out; and when he is come, he findeth it empty, swept, and garnished.

**45 Then goeth he, and taketh with himself seven other spir-
its more wicked than himself, and they enter in and dwell
there: and the last state of that man is worse than the first.
Even so shall it be also unto this wicked generation.**

Because they find no rest in the dry places, they
seek living beings to inhabit. Demonic spirits, therefore,
desire a living host in which to dwell. It might be worth-
while to note that in this passage of scripture, Jesus was
speaking to scribes and Pharisees, the most religious
people of the land.

As a believer in the Lord Jesus Christ, you must know
without a shadow of a doubt, that you are covered with
the blood of Jesus, and no demon, fallen angel, or evil spirit can penetrate the blood of Jesus. You need not fear
because you have authority through the blood of Jesus, the
finished work of Calvary. No evil being has authority or
dominion over you in Jesus' Name. Hallelujah!

Jesus encountered demonic beings on several
recorded occasions, and no doubt many that were not
recorded. One such occasion was in Gadara, just after
He had quieted the raging storm on the Sea of Galilee.
He and His disciples came upon a naked, demon possessed man who lived in caves.

After Jesus commanded the demons to come out of
the man, He let them go into a herd of swine. Demonic
beings desire living beings through which they work, so
the residents of Gadara were unknowingly blessed by the
work of Jesus. Those demons could just as easily have
gone into human hosts. So you see, demons can work
either through a human body or through an animal.

You might also notice that when Jesus exercised
authority and cast out the demons, He experienced great
resistance and antagonism from the Gadarenes. The
Gadarenes had heard how Jesus cast out demons from

the demoniac, restoring him to his rightful mind. They knew that the swine had hurled themselves into the sea and drowned. Yet, instead of rejoicing that the man was set free, they asked Jesus to leave.

Demons Identify Themselves

On another occasion described in Matthew 12:22-37, a demon possessed man who was blind and mute was brought to Jesus. After the man was healed, the people marveled. Then the Pharisees entered into the picture, saying that He had cast out the devils by Beelzebub. These religious people could not deny the results, so they attacked the source of His power. Jesus was the Truth and the Light; and where truth prevails, it demands honesty.

When the Pharisees said of Jesus, that He was of Beelzebub, they were identifying themselves. Because of the light and truth being present in Jesus, they were compelled to name themselves and who rules over them. The same thing happens to us when someone lashes out evil railings toward us. They are declaring what they are and what is in them. Matthew 12:35 says, "A good man out of the good treasure of the heart bringeth forth good things: and an evil man out of the evil treasure bringeth forth evil things."

This brings to mind an experience that happened one evening, during Intercessors' 500 (an annual conference focused on prayer and sponsored by A Great Love). I was making my way to one of the evening meetings. As my friend and I stepped into the elevator, I saw a man dressed in a tuxedo also occupying the elevator. Obviously he was on his way to a formal function at the hotel.

After the service ended, I was once again waiting for the elevator. When the door opened, I was astonished to find the same man at the rear of the elevator. Accompanying him this time to his left, were two very drunk women. I stepped into the elevator and turned to face the doors, when to my right I noticed two young men, possibly in their early twenties.

After the doors closed and the elevator was moving, the young man nearest to me leaned over and said, "Hare Krishna." I felt like a vigorously shaken can of soda pop that someone had just opened. Without a second thought, five words simply bubbled out with authority and boldness, yet dignified and calm. I answered him with, "Not Hare Krishna, Jesus Christ." Dead silence hit that elevator as it climbed to its destination.

The next afternoon I shared this peculiar experience with one of our helps ministers who ministers in the streets of his home city and regularly works in our conferences. He said, "I know exactly what it was. That happens to me all the time. That demon in him was naming himself, and he was calling you what he is, but he was naming himself." Immediately I remembered Matthew 12, that warns us to guard what we call other people, because the very thing that we call them, is probably what is in us.

Python Is Exposed

My younger son, Dan, and I were ministering in a very rustic area of Alaska, when I was confronted with strong manifestations of wickedness in high places. They most assuredly were not flesh and blood. The Spirit of God wanted to move, but it was like a brazen wall that was impenetrable. I felt like I had been swept back in time for an undeterminable number of years.

During the first meeting, the Holy Spirit gave some words of knowledge which were received. I knew it was to be a sign to the people in attendance. They needed to know the power of Jesus and the Holy Spirit in manifestation. Because of the anointing, I recognize when there is, or is not, a free flow of the Holy Spirit. The Spirit was definitely not free flowing although the people wanted a glorious manifestation of the presence of God, and so did I.

All through that night, I was burdened. The following morning I sat down on the floor next to my bed, took my Bible in hand, and cried out, "Lord, show me what these people and I are up against." You see, wherever I minister, I want to be on target and minister in such a manner that the people's lives will be transformed. I want to be in God's perfect will so that the people can be blessed beyond their imagination. When I came up against this resistance in the spirit, I needed to find out from the Lord what was happening.

As I sought the Lord and prayed in the Holy Spirit, God began to minister to me. He showed me the ruling spirit over that area. Then He took me to the Scriptures and showed me the operation of this ruling spirit, as well as some of its cohorts and how they operated. Often we pray against the fruit of evil or against the minor skirmishes, without targeting the ruling spirit. I wrote, prayed, and read the Word of God at length and didn't say a word except to take authority over things that were revealed.

The ministers that had invited us to come, were a stable mature Christian couple with a bona fide call of God to apostle a work in that area. Try as they would, they had overwhelming opposition on every hand. The only building they were able to acquire was the use of a high school, and even that was limited to one weekly service. I knew there had to be an answer to such great oppression.

I saw that rebellion was a strong characteristic of the area. When rebellious people settled there from the lower forty-eight states, they brought their rebellion with them. Many had also been escaped convicts and law breakers. After discussing this with the pastor and his wife, they confirmed what I had received from the Lord.

Another pastoral couple in that same area had been there for thirty years, and experienced the same kind of struggle and opposition. Their church would grow nicely for a while, and then things would fall apart, and they would seemingly have to start all over again. I shared with them what I received about the ruling spirit. The pastor and his wife wholeheartedly agreed that it was so.

In the city areas, child molestation and incest were rampant. Our host pastor and his wife also made mention of a Russian village nearby where alcoholism, incestuous marriages, child abuse of all kinds, and other horrible abuses were commonplace. Apparently many settlers that crossed over from the Soviet Union settled in that area and it has remained somewhat isolated.

As soon as they told me about this village, I just knew that I had to go there. I was told that the villagers preferred their isolation and were especially suspicious towards strangers coming into their village. I insisted that I wanted to go regardless of any possible danger.

That following Saturday, our host pastor, his wife, my son Dan, and I were off on our way to that Russian village. As we arrived, there was a tremendous sense of the prevailing spirits in the atmosphere. There was an aura of dirty, dingy, darkness. The road was a dirt road, the houses were squalid, and it even smelled of filth.

The most impressive structure in the entire village was the Russian Orthodox Church.

As we were driving along, I was told the story of another village similar to the one we were visiting. Apparently a minister traveling on his way to another destination had to pass through the village. As he was passing through, he stopped. The priest of the Orthodox church approached him and threatened him with death if he were not out of the village by sundown. The story was told as an example of the hostile attitudes of the region.

Antagonism is something that all of us encounter at some point. People who cause division, speak evil about you, or come against you in other ways, simply do not know what they are doing. They are blinded by the god of this world (2 Corinthians).

Our response to such matters should be, "Forgive them, Father, and open their eyes. Remove the blinders from them by the power of the Holy Spirit and the blood of the Lord Jesus Christ."

I believe as never before, the church of America is coming to the realization that it is in a war. Jesus is enlisting in His army, those who will listen to the Holy Spirit, those who will not care about man-pleasing, and those who are not trusting the arm of flesh. They will be ready for the persecution and warfare.

While driving through this oppressed village, there were some people milling about outside. The moment the residents spotted us, they dashed into their houses, and in a short time there was no one left on the streets. As we drove through the area, we were all praying in tongues. I took authority over the oppressive spirit of religion that held the village by the throat and was choking the life out of it.

The results of revealing the ruling spirit and its three companion cohorts of that area to our host pastor and his wife were glorious. They went to war in the realm of the spirit and became overcomers. Their church began to grow and now they have their own church building.

Not only did they break those powers that were keeping them from fulfilling their vision, they are maintaining their victory through prayer. In addition, I received a report that the priest of the Russian Orthodox church in the village we visited, is now born again, and has led members of his congregation to the Lord Jesus Christ. To God be the glory!

Be About the Father's Business

Frequently believers have the impression that demonic spiritual manifestations occurring in other nations and on other continents are not occurring here in the United States. The rude awakening, however, is that there is an extremely large number of occurrences right here. The worst kind of deception is that of denial.

Having traveled to foreign nations in the ministry, I have had to deal with witchcraft directly. I've broken the curse of death over people who would have been dead the next day because of the workings of witch doctors. In open air crusades, I have removed amulets from children that have been put on them by charmers. These things are commonplace in nations outside this country, but I must tell you that we in this nation must wake up to the growth and spread of witchcraft and the occult.

God is giving us the revelation of ruling spirits so that we can do something about it.

ROMANS 5:21

21 That as sin hath reigned unto death, even so might grace reign through righteousness unto eternal life by Jesus Christ our Lord.

We do not have to be afraid of these things, but rather be busy about the Father's business as Jesus was. "...For this purpose the Son of God was manifested, that he might destroy the works of the devil" (1 John 3:8b).

I once asked a minister friend to tell me the number one spirit that operates against him as he ministers in the nations of Africa. He responded, "The spirit of religion, that's the hardest spirit to overcome." Without a doubt, this is the reason that the religious people gave Jesus the most opposition, the greatest antagonism, and were so easily used by demonic forces to bring about His crucifixion.

1 CORINTHIANS 2:8

8 Which none of the princes of this world knew: for had they known it, they would not have crucified the Lord of glory.

Python In Operation

Who are the princes of this world? In the 16th chapter of Acts, Paul is found ministering in Macedonia. It says, "And it came to pass, as we went to prayer, a certain damsel possessed with a spirit of divination met us, which brought her masters much gain by soothsaying" (Acts 16:16). The spirit of divination is referred to as a spirit of Python (middle column reference) in The Holy Bible, Cambridge University Press, for example.

The word python comes from the Greek word "puthon" and is connected with the cult of Apollo in ancient Greece. In Greek mythology, Python was a serpent that guarded the oracle of Delphi on Mt. Pernassus.

This serpent was slain by Apollo, who then took on the name Apollo Pythius. Diviners and soothsayers of old were associated with the cult of Apollo, and therefore operated in a spirit of python.

Acts 16:16 reveals the ruling spirit, the python spirit. What is a python? It is a powerful constricting snake that squeezes its prey to death. Examples are the boa and anaconda. Just like the snake, the spirit of python wraps itself around its victims and strangulates the life out of them. It works against believers today, just as it did against Paul in Macedonia.

When you go to prayer, you are entering into the realm of the supernatural to possess the land for Almighty God. That spirit of divination, alias spirit of python, goes to battle against you. Manifestations of this spirit in action are weariness, fatigue, confusion, and frustration.

When this spirit is operating against a church, home, business, or ministry, it begins to squeeze people out. People can't seem to stay because of the pressure, oppression, depression, and heaviness. Yet it will continue to constrict until there are divisions, factions, and discouragement, which is the fruit of a spirit of python.

Confronting Python

I was at a convention in Oklahoma, where I met a particular pastor. The Spirit of the Lord spoke to me and instructed me that I should go to his church to minister. I didn't know the size of his church or anything else about it. For all I knew, it could have been a church of ten or ten thousand people. In the meantime, the Lord had also spoken to him, and instructed him to invite me. During the last evening service of the convention, he made his way to where I was seated and asked me to come to his church, which was in the San Diego area. I readily agreed, knowing that the Holy Spirit was orchestrating something.

I had been to California numerous times over a seven year period, and there had always been mighty anointings upon me as I ministered. There was no reason to think this time would be any different.

The morning after my arrival in California for this series of meetings (which included the San Diego area church), I awakened with an unshakable heavy burden. Even intercession didn't seem to bring release. When I cried out to the Lord for the people of that area of California, I saw that a line had been drawn. Even though I didn't fully understand the reason for the line, I knew that God's people were standing on that line. I also knew that if they did not make the right decision, it would be disastrous. They urgently had to choose God's side of the line.

This burden remained with me, and I just could not seem to shake it. I saw in part, knew in part, but was not able to get the totality of it. I listened to what other people were saying so that I could hear by the Spirit of the Lord in confirmation, revelation, or more illumination about circumstances in California at that time, which concerned the church of the Lord Jesus Christ.

The Bible says that we are not to be ignorant of the devices of Satan. I had never been known to specifically deal in deliverance, or even to minister on topics about the devil, but it was time to awaken and know about the battle. After this trip to California, I knew beyond any doubt that the church of America was in a war.

After a week's ministry in the Los Angeles area, I was scheduled to minister in Beverly Hills. Meeting with the pastor of the church, I asked him what he was hearing from the Spirit of the Lord. He told me that he was about to ask me the same thing. So, I began to discuss what I had perceived.

He then shared with me that a very well known and highly respected pastor in the area was confirming the fact that people needed to give heed to prophecies of impending catastrophe. The line had been drawn and people needed to hear from the Lord as to where He wanted them to live.

For years, prophecies have been given about California dropping off into the sea and other great disasters occurring. I have come to the conclusion that these are prophets who are seeing things that will happen when God pours out his wrath upon the earth, but these prophets are making the mistake of putting a fixed time frame on it. Primarily, setting dates and times should be avoided. Just let God be God, and go about doing His work.

On Thursday evening, I ministered in Beverly Hills as planned. Present at that meeting was a very precious God-given friend of mine, who is a well seasoned veteran in the ministry. She worked closely with Aimee Semple McPherson and has founded many churches herself. I did not have the opportunity to speak to her that evening, but I phoned her the next morning.

When I asked her what the Lord was showing her, she responded by telling me that when I began to flow in the Spirit during the prior evening's service, she had wept uncontrollably. I knew she had seen things in the spirit realm. She was in full agreement as I explained about the line I had seen, and that I did not have the full revelation of it yet.

She then shared with me that during one of her services, a high priest of Satan was in attendance. Afterwards, he approached her saying, "I have been sent by Satan, and I am here to tell you that we have marked 500 leading ministers in this area, including pastors, television and radio ministers of the Los Angeles area. We have marked them for death and destruction, and you are one of them."

Well, you might have thought she was discussing a birthday party. This saint of God was not moved in the least by these threats. Since that time, she had already found two black cats at her doorstep, with their throats slit.

Others have suffered terrible fates. A well known television minister with a large church, one day simply walked away from it. A couple who had been teaching marriage seminars all over the country suddenly divorced. This is not flesh and blood in operation, but rather demonic spirits.

On the following Sunday I ministered at the San Diego area church. As I ministered in the morning service, there was a precious move of the Holy Spirit. The evening service was quite a different story. I had heard that California was a manufacturer of fruits, flakes, and nuts. However, to the contrary, my experience in ministering there had always found the people solid and anointed.

That evening I departed for the church rejoicing and feeling great. As I was ushered into the church office, I saw others there seated in a circle praying. I was seated on a chair directly opposite from the pastor. Everyone was diligently praying, when suddenly I felt something ominous.

I saw a black cloud-like force coming from the pastor's direction towards me. I felt like it was trying to enter me. I knew if it did, it would crush and smother me. Taking my stand against it with the blood of Jesus and in His Name, I commanded it saying, "You can't enter me!"

I was puzzled why it had come from the pastor's direction. Since I really did not know this man, you can be sure I was testing the spirits after this startling experience. The pastor came over to me and said, "You know, I'm totally puzzled. Right before you came in, did you get anything about me?"

Since I hadn't, not that I didn't want to, I responded with a simple, "No."

He said, "Right before you came, a darkness came over me. Inside it's like I want to...." He was so puzzled and torn inside, he couldn't express himself. I didn't dare tell him what I had just experienced, because I didn't know what it was.

Obviously the evil darkness of this world did not want the evening service to be as wonderful, or even greater, than the morning service had been. Having prayed, and being alert, we went into the sanctuary.

The praise and worship was glorious. The song of the Holy Spirit went forth and the worship was so anointed, it was truly marvelous. Suddenly, as if somebody had cut off the water supply, the worship team ended this glorious worship. They then tried to lead into another direction.

The Lord had just spoken to me, telling me, "I want you to come up higher. If you don't come up higher, you can't see the things that I want you to see up here." Well, I was certainly ready to go up higher and see what He had for me.

The worship team tried, but it was as uninspired as you can imagine. It was downright dead! I was so puzzled that one moment there was glory, and the next moment it was gone. I prayed, "O Lord, why didn't they stay in the Spirit? Why don't they flow in the Spirit?" I felt if they did, they would have the most wondrous operation of the Holy Spirit.

When the pastor realized that they were immobilized, he then tried everything he could, but it was still dampened. Then a woman gave a word of the Lord that was on target, and it charged the atmosphere.

No sooner did she finish, when a man from the back of the church spoke out. It was the kind of utterance that makes you immediately say, "What is that?" It was fruits, flakes, and nuts, all rolled up together. I turned to see who was giving that off-the-wall thing right from the flesh and the enemy. Several people suddenly began to behave like a box of cereal that was knocked over, and everything came pouring out.

The church became like a three-ring circus with the performers in competition for attention. One after another, they performed. I had never seen anything like it before, and really don't want to again.

When nobody else could do anything, they decided that it was time for me to minister, so they called me forward. It was just that morning that I had given a marvelous teaching on grace that flowed like the river of the Holy Ghost. That evening was another story.

I opened my Bible and fully intended to minister a closing message on grace, but then I simply closed my Bible. I said, "As the ole pastor responded when asked about the anointing, 'I don't exactly know what the anointing is, but I know when it ain't,' and it isn't here now." I further said, "I am not playing church. I am not pretending. I am going back to the hotel; I'm going to rest; I'm going to pack; and I'm going to leave tomorrow. And you're going home."

There was a man seated in the front row who was a warrior in intercession, and I said to him, "If this can be broken, we're going to break it." I found myself recharged by these bold declarations.

With that, a man of questionable stability slammed his Bible shut, and in a great huff, stormed out of the church. I was told later that he does that frequently. He apparently goes to meetings where the Spirit of God is moving, and acts up like that. His behavior was typical of what was going on there that night.

As I was summoning the intercessor to come forward and lead in prayer, I went to the pastor to ask him if he had anything to add or say. He said that he didn't, and continued to sit where he was.

Again, I stepped up to him and asked him if he had any discernment as to the source of all this disturbance. He answered, "You named it when you prayed. You bound the spirit of python. That's it. That's the ruling spirit."

What I did not know at this time was that on the Thursday night prior to this service, a prophet was ministering to the congregation. That prophet told them that within three days another prophet would come, and without any prior knowledge about this word, would identify the ruling spirit over that area and the church. The third day was Sunday, and I was the mouthpiece used of the Lord to identify that ruling spirit.

When the pastor spoke those words, I knew we had it. I was on fire and ready for action. I asked the intercessor to lead the warfare in overcoming its operations.

Demons don't like to be identified by believers moving in authority. Before I stepped aside, the same man who gave the first weird utterance that set everybody off, stood up and said, "I've got the answer. I've got the revelation." Then he spouted off another string of nonsense.

With that, I boldly declared to the congregation, "I want everybody in here to follow this intercessor, and the Spirit of God." Then I told the disruptive man to sit down and keep quiet in Jesus' Name. The next time I looked, he was gone.

A holy boldness took over, and the battle was full steam ahead. At one point, the enemy stepped onto my shoulder and said, "Just wait until they hear about this!" I refused to be intimidated.

All I did was reaffirm to God, "Father, I didn't start this, and I'm not going to finish it. I'm getting out of the way. You started it, and You will finish it." Before the night was over, the spirit of python was broken over that area.

Prior to all of these events, this church continually struggled. They were not able to rent any other building, so they rented the second floor of an office building. They experienced split after split. When I arrived, they had only fifty people in their congregation. There was no rational reason for their conflicts.

The pastor and his wife were doing what they knew to do, yet it was a continuous struggle. Best friends turned on them; people who they thought were mature turned out to be babes; associates ran off with groups of people. It was the worst case scenario of everything that could go wrong.

After that spirit was broken, another pastor in that area who had a lovely church located on acres of land, phoned them and said, "I'm really not a pastor, I'm an evangelist. Please bring your congregation and take this church, so that I can go out to evangelize." I was told that there had never been a history of revival in the San Diego area. Now the revival fires have been lit.

The War is Raging

Jesus came to set people free from the powers of all evil and darkness. Liberty is one of the major fruits of His sacrifice.

JOHN 8:36

36 If the Son therefore shall make you free, ye shall be free indeed.

JOHN 8: 31b-32

31 ...If ye continue in my word, then are ye my disciples indeed;

32 And ye shall know the truth, and the truth shall make you free.

The work of the Holy Spirit is one of freedom and liberty. Second Corinthians 3:17 says, "Now the Lord is that Spirit: and where the Spirit of the Lord is, there is liberty." The literal Greek meaning of this verse indicates that where the Holy Spirit is Lord, there is liberty.

Religion, in its most literal sense, means a return to bondage. Is it any wonder that we are exhorted to, "Stand fast therefore in the liberty wherewith Christ hath made us free, and be not entangled again with the yoke of bondage" (Galatians 5:1).

Religion is only one element of Satan's trinity, which is the spirit of python, religion, and the spirit of divination. The devil is fighting to keep us from our jubilee, that is, the liberty of Jesus Christ in the perfection of divine order in our homes, businesses, and churches.

In Sweden, there is a great apostolic work that is under continuous fire and harassment. The state church released a large sum of *Krona* to participate in the stopping of that work. The government actively opposes them. Satanic attacks are set up to operate against them.

The pastor of this Swedish church has awakened to find a circle of blood and mutilated animals around his home. He finds defaming slurs written on his house. His church is in warfare, and it's no Saturday morning cartoon. With knowledge of such warfare comes the responsibility to defeat the strategies and schemes of the adversary.

I shared with this Swedish pastor about seeing the line drawn in California. This is not flaky stuff; this is reality. He said that satanists are all over the world marking their lines and learning to tap into the spirit world of evil. They are setting up territorial domains within lines marked in the spirit by satanic powers.

I was astonished to find out that in Elberton, Georgia, just fifty miles from my home town, there is a monument that is visited annually by satanic worshippers engaging in occultish activities. It is supposedly the center of the earth and has some ritualistic meaning to them. The work of the enemy is global and real.

New Agers use the rainbow as a symbol, claiming that it is a covenant symbol for them. They have perverted God's covenant that He spoke to Noah.

GENESIS 9:11-17

11 And I will establish my covenant with you; neither shall all flesh be cut off any more by the waters of a flood; neither shall there any more be a flood to destroy the earth.

12 And God said, This is the token of the covenant which I make between me and you and every living creature that is with you, for perpetual generations:

13 I do set my bow in the cloud, and it shall be for a token of a covenant between me and the earth.

14 And it shall come to pass, when I bring a cloud over the earth, that the bow shall be seen in the cloud:

15 And I will remember my covenant, which is between me and you and every living creature of all flesh; and the waters shall no more become a flood to destroy all flesh.

16 And the bow shall be in the cloud; and I will look upon it, that I may remember the everlasting covenant between

God and every living creature of all flesh that is upon the earth.

17 And God said unto Noah, This is the token of the covenant, which I have established between me and all flesh that is upon the earth.

God confirmed this Noahic covenant in Isaiah 54. The devil has perverted the true rainbow of God, the covenant of God, and has given it to some of his followers. Therefore, the New Agers, and others, promote this perversion of the rainbow covenant symbol, thinking that Almighty God, Creator of heaven and earth, is in what they do.

Pastor friends of mine in Washington, D.C., were seeking the Lord regarding the ruling spirit over that city. They repeatedly witnessed ministers beginning works and then being squeezed out of them. Division and competition are greatly evident as some seemingly are trying to build their own kingdoms. These pastor friends received from God, that the ruling spirit over Washington, D.C., was a spirit of python.

Could the ruling spirit over this nation be the spirit of python? Every revival we have ever had, including Azuza Street, was powerful and explosive from the beginning, growing by leaps and bounds. Then suddenly, the revival light was squeezed out of it. That is the work of python.

We see in Acts 16 the spirit of python was primarily trying to stop the spread of the gospel of the Lord Jesus Christ into all the world. When Paul and Silas stepped onto the second continent to bring the gospel, a python spirit instantly went to war against them.

Will we, the church of America, break the power of the python spirit over our churches, ministries, homes, places of work, and over our nation? In Macedonia, when Paul broke this ruling spirit's power by the authority given by Jesus, multitudes came to the Lord. Let us want to break the power of this ruling spirit and see the multitudes come to God.

Other spirits that work with the spirit of python, religion, and divination are manipulative spirits, controlling spirits, beguiling spirits, seducing spirits, and the Jezebel spirit. The ruling spirit, however, is python. It can work in money matters, squeezing the life out of people who are trying to give finances into the spreading of the gospel of the Lord Jesus Christ. It attempts to squeeze money, the anointing, and anything good or profitable, out of churches, ministers, and everything it touches.

We must break its power in Jesus' Name. Then we must maintain in intercession what we gain in intercession to fulfill the good, acceptable, and perfect will of God in our lives as believers.

Chapter 2
Reality of Python

As we obey God and His Word, darkness is exposed. The light of God's Word and the work of the Holy Spirit swallows up the darkness. Knowing the circumstances surrounding your life, you can take what is in the Word of God, and become more discerning. The authority that has been given to believers by Jesus Christ can be exercised to bring forth results.

The devil is under the believer's legal authority in Christ Jesus within the realm of what God has decreed. When a believer approaches him, and takes authority over him on the basis of the finished work of Calvary, he has no choice but to submit.

GALATIANS 3:13,14

13 Christ hath redeemed us from the curse of the law, being made a curse for us: for it is written, Cursed is every one that hangeth on a tree:

14 That the blessing of Abraham might come on the Gentiles through Jesus Christ; that we might receive the promise of the Spirit through faith.

You must remind the devil that the blood of Jesus Christ has been shed for you, and His precious blood covers everything that concerns you. The devil hates the blood of Jesus because he knows the power of that blood. That is why pagans throughout the course of human history, and those practicing demonic rituals of witchcraft today, engage in blood sacrifices. They are seeking power that cannot come from any source other than the precious blood of the Lord Jesus Christ. In his usual strategies, the devil influences his own to seek and function with a counterfeit.

We need to have a great appreciation, understanding, faith, and confidence in the accomplishments of the precious blood of Jesus Christ. By faith in the Name of Jesus, the Son of God, we must boldly proclaim what the blood of Jesus and the authority of His Name has been given to do. We must have confidence in the grace of God, His ability, power, strength, efficiency, and sufficiency, that is working on our behalf.

If you have never exercised His authority, pray for God to give you a spirit of boldness. Begin to allow the Spirit of God to lead your spirit, because the devil does not acknowledge authority in one who just knows about God. We must know Him! We need to understand that we are the temple of God, purchased by the blood of Jesus, and the enemy has no authority to enter.

When you battle the enemy, use the weapons of the Cross, the blood of Jesus, the Word of God, and the authority of the Name of Jesus. In Matthew 12:43, Jesus says that demons who have been cast out walk around in dry places seeking rest, but they find none. They then go back to the "house" from which they were driven. If a demon finds his former house empty, devoid of the Spirit of God and the living reality of the Word of God, he calls seven of his pals to join him in a house-warming party.

When this demon joins up with seven more wicked ones, there are then eight demons where there once was only one. The number eight, in the Bible, indicates new beginnings. When those eight demons enter their host, their new beginnings are even more powerful than the first, and consequently, the person is far worse off.

You can see the importance of filling a person with the Spirit and the Word of God once they have been delivered. In order to maintain their deliverance, the person needs to grow in faith and grace, renewing their mind with the Word of God. They can then continue to live a victorious life.

Overcoming the Ruling Spirit

During one of our Intercessors' 500 meetings, we saw a graphic illustration of this principle. There was a great demonstration of God in setting homosexuals and lesbians free. A young man who once had been set free had willingly opened the door to this again. When he did, he unknowingly invited a whole team of demons back into his life.

During the service, there was a powerful move of God and people were falling under the power of the Holy Spirit in sections all over the room. This young man came forward for help. He desperately wanted deliverance.

Did you know that you can actually smell demonic activity? There is a foul odor of death and sin, and under the anointing you can actually smell the putrid stench of demonic presence. In contrast, is the sweet smelling fragrance of Almighty God upon His people (2 Corinthians 2:14-16). This young man, however, was not smelling sweet, but rather, the odor that was emitting from him was almost unbearable.

At this point it was late in the evening, almost midnight, and this young man was now on the floor, which did not mean that he had been delivered from anything. It only meant that he could not stand in the Presence of

God. Deliverance had not really been something that I did at these kinds of meetings. In fact, this was a first at Intercessors' 500.

When the demons acted up around Jesus, He did not say, "Will you please wait just a little longer, and we'll go to the back room of the synagogue. We don't want to disturb the congregation, and we certainly don't want to embarrass anyone." No, right there with the demon possessed person foaming at the mouth, acting in all kinds of bizarre mannerisms, Jesus immediately attended to it and set him free.

Just like the woman who was bowed over for eighteen years, the bondage was long enough and she needed to be free right then and there. In Luke 13:15,16 Jesus answered the religious rulers who took offense over the fact that she was healed on the sabbath,

LUKE 13:15,16

15 ...Thou hypocrite, doth not each one of you on the sabbath loose his ox or his ass from the stall, and lead him away to watering?

16 And ought not this woman, being a daughter of Abraham, whom Satan hath bound, lo, these eighteen years, be loosed from this bond on the sabbath day?

We prayed and cast out various demons from this young man, but there was still another one. I saw Glenda, my daughter-in-law, standing on the platform. I called her to come because of her anointing. I said, "Glenda, that demon is wanting attention."

With total composure, she said, "I have received one word, control. It's a spirit of control." She ministered to the young man, and he was totally set free.

The ruling spirit was hiding behind the other demons, controlling them as well as the young man. He did not want to come out of his comfortable house. Sometimes the other demonic spirits are protecting that ruling spirit. When I shared that with my younger son, Dan, he responded in his usual practical way. He said, "Well, in the army, they don't put the leader out front first because they don't want him to get shot. They protect him and put all the others on the front lines first." In that way, the strategist can continue his work. It seems simple enough.

Recognizing Demons

Many years ago, I asked the Lord how I would be able to tell when somebody has a demon. He told me, "Along with the gift of discerning of spirits, look into their eyes. You can tell by their eyes whether or not they have a demon." Well, I found that very interesting. The Bible says much about eyes, and apparently it is a sense gate through which truth is perceived from both sides, the one looking out as well as the one looking in. Jesus says, in Luke 11:34, "The light of the body is the eye: therefore when thine eye is single, thy whole body also is full of light; but when thine eye is evil, thy body also is full of darkness."

A few years prior to this other incident, I was in Jamaica ministering. When I thought the service had ended, the pastor stood up and announced that some people had brought a woman into the service, and they wanted me to pray for her. I went back to the platform and was shocked at what I saw. Four men dragged a woman forward, who looked like a pathetic rag doll.

When the anointing of God begins to stir inside, you get very bold and strong as a lion. Demons cannot cross the blood line and faith rises up. This is not a game and nothing with which to become fascinated. Demons want attention, so don't enter into a conversation with them, just cast them out.

As those men stood the woman up before me, I began to get angry inside, in the same way that Jesus was angry and drove out the moneychangers from the temple. Sympathy has no place in this situation. I was not dealing with flesh and blood. This woman was no worse off than someone with a disease. The demonic spirits just needed to be cast out and she would be made whole.

Jesus is our example. He simply addressed the demonic spirit and commanded it to leave. When it left, the person was made whole. It's just another part of the business of helping people to get free and live in the kingdom of God.

It took four men to hold up that limp woman. I took authority over the situation and God showed me the nature of what held her in bondage. She had the curse of a spirit of death put upon her by a worker of witchcraft. If something didn't happen very soon, she would die.

I told the men to let her go. They looked at me like I was crazy, so again I told them to let go of her. Hesitatingly, they released her, and I commanded her to stand.

She refused to look at me, so I pried open her eyelids to look into her eyes. There was blood in her eyes. Now I don't mean bloodshot as one who is fatigued. There was a feisty demon staring back at me.

I commanded that spirit of death to come out of her in the Name of Jesus. That demon had to come out. I wouldn't let her close her eyes. Then I walked with her up and down the aisles. When it was finished, the Lord Jesus Christ had totally delivered that woman.

Her story then revealed that a witch doctor had indeed placed a curse of death upon her. She became born again, and that next Sunday, along with many others, was baptized in the Caribbean Sea, to the glory of God.

The following year I was back in Jamaica for a New Year's Eve service and some scheduled weeks of ministry. A Great Love had purchased a tent for this pastor so that he could travel over the island and minister. This was my first tent meeting.

It was nearing the midnight hour, and I turned the meeting back over to the pastor thinking he would like to usher in the new year with his congregation. Then I sat down at my seat on the platform, as the pastor came forward to the pulpit.

When the pastor announced the arrival of the new year, a woman got up from her seat, and gently walked down the aisle. She came before the pulpit and knelt down on the sawdust floor. Raising her hands and face, she worshipped in such a manner, that the glory of God was all over her.

The pastor's wife tapped me and asked, "You know who that is, don't you?"

I didn't know the woman, so I answered, "No."

She said, "She is the one that you cast the demon of death out of, and she has a lot to be grateful for."

Jesus set her free! I do not have a "deliverance" ministry. I trust God that by His grace, I have a Jesus ministry, where I am about my Father's business.

MARK 16:17,18

16 And these signs shall follow them that believe; In my name shall they cast out devils; they shall speak with new tongues;

17 They shall take up serpents; and if they drink any deadly thing, it shall not hurt them; they shall lay hands on the sick, and they shall recover.

Casting out devils is as much a sign as speaking in tongues or laying hands on the sick, and seeing them recover. It says that these are the signs that follow the *believer.*

We must not allow ourselves to become demon chasers, fascinated by their manifestations, and specializing in this one area of the working of signs. Don't think that just because someone has bloodshot eyes, he needs a demon cast out of him.

On the other hand we can't go to the other extreme and deny their existence and operation on the earth. We need to be open to the Holy Spirit, and He will reveal things to us. We need to prayerfully seek balance in our walk in the Spirit. Proverbs 11:1 says, "A false balance is abomination to the Lord: but a just weight is his delight."

Paul's Experience

What is divination? Simply stated, it is a superstitious method of trying to discover the course of future events or causing them to happen by superstitious means. Whenever a spirit of divination (python) is in operation, there will be false prophesying, and a profit motive somewhere in operation.

ACTS 16:16-26

16 And it came to pass, as we went to prayer, a certain damsel possessed with a spirit of divination met us, which brought her masters much gain by soothsaying:

17 The same followed Paul and us, and cried, saying, These men are the servants of the most high God, which shew unto us the way of salvation.

18 And this did she many days. But Paul, being grieved, turned and said to the spirit, I command thee in the name of Jesus Christ to come out of her. And he came out the same hour.

19 And when her masters saw that the hope of their gains was gone, they caught Paul and Silas, and drew them into the marketplace unto the rulers,

20 And brought them to the magistrates, saying, These men, being Jews, do exceedingly trouble our city,

21 And teach customs, which are not lawful for us to receive, neither to observe, being Romans.

22 And the multitude rose up together against them: and the magistrates rent off their clothes, and commanded to beat them.

23 And when they had laid many stripes upon them, they cast them into prison, charging the jailer to keep them safely:

24 Who, having received such a charge, thrust them into the inner prison, and made their feet fast in the stocks.

25 And at midnight Paul and Silas prayed, and sang praises unto God: and the prisoners heard them.

26 And suddenly there was a great earthquake, so that the foundations of the prison were shaken: and immediately all the doors were opened, and every one's bands were loosed.

This occurred in Philippi, Macedonia, the first place Paul ministered in Europe. Notice that it was not just the bands of Paul and Silas which were loosed after praying and singing praises, but everyone's bands.

The Money Motive

In verse 16, we see that the operation of the spirit of python (divination), always has money attached to it. The masters of this demon possessed girl were making a profit from her fortune-telling.

The way that python operates against individuals in their home, business, or church finances, is that he constricts the flow of finances. He prevents business deals from closing in your favor. He prevents the sale of houses, or lands. He dries up the funds from a church, because he knows without it, the ministry cannot go on.

As with the damsel in Paul's experience there will always be these two elements, forecasting future events and "much gain by soothsaying." We have witches in our own nation who call themselves "prophetesses". They dabble in a variety of fortune-telling methods, using paraphernalia related to the occult.

A pastor and his wife, who are friends of mine, were invited to minister at another church. They were given directions from their hotel that indicated the church was near a house with a sign that read, "Prophetess Mary." The pastor, being a man of wisdom and experience, had insight into what kind of prophetess she was.

He found his way to the church and stood before the congregation to minister the Word of God. Instead of preaching, he announced, "Saints, I cannot minister the Word of God to you until I first go and minister the gospel of our Lord Jesus Christ to Prophetess Mary." With that he walked off the platform, and left a Sunday morning congregation sitting in wonder.

When he arrived at Prophetess Mary's door, he knocked and identified himself. She let him in and took him into her "back room." There were little candles lit along side of a crucifix on an altar. She declared, "I say the Lord's prayer every day."

Having a form of religion was not enough for salvation. She did not receive Jesus as her Lord and Savior. Like the damsel in Paul's story, she was involved in divination with a profit motive. She was a "profitess," not a prophetess.

False Prophesying

Learning to distinguish fact from fiction, reality from fantasy, and in this case, truth from falsehood, is at times very subtle. Acts 16:17 tells us exactly what the young girl was saying. "The same followed Paul and us, and cried, saying, These men are the servants of the most high God, which shew unto us the way of salvation." At first glance you would think she was absolutely correct. What could be wrong with her statement?

Proverbs 14:12 says, "There is a way which seemeth right unto a man, but the end thereof are the ways of death." Satan comes as an angel of light. It is so close to the light that it takes the pure light of the Lord Jesus Christ to reveal it for the darkness that it is.

Notice the words, "unto us" in Acts 16:17, by which the young girl is referring to the local people including herself. She recognized the call, anointing, and message of Paul and Silas. What she was saying about Paul and Silas was designed to give her credibility in the eyes of the local people, so that after the apostles were gone, she would have a built-in following. The people would believe anything she said thinking that she possessed prophetic power.

In her declaring, "They have come to show us the way of salvation," she was being controlled. The spirit of python was working in her to squeeze out life. What she said was so close to the truth, yet the absolute opposite. The clue is that she was glorifying Paul and Silas instead of Jesus.

This is how the devil works. In seeming to be right, deception is actually at work. Because she was a follower of the apostles while they were present, it would also seem right for others to follow her and her evil psychic abilities after they were gone.

It is vitally important for us to know those who labor among us, as we are admonished in 1 Thessalonians 5:12. We must know their character when they are not in the public limelight. They may say things that seem right, and everything could look great on the surface, but that is not the test of their spiritual maturity. The fruit of the Holy Spirit needs to be evident in their lives.

Attacking the Authority, Mantle, and Call

From this account in Acts 16, we can see other ways that python operates. Paul was the one who was sent to Philippi with the message of salvation. He had the authority, mantle, and call for that work of God. This young woman had followed Paul and Silas around for days, making proclamations about them, giving them her seal of approval. It gave the local population the idea that they had the same mystical agenda as this young woman. However, what she was really doing, was breaking down God's divine order of authority, mantle, and calling.

The python spirit has as its goal, the breaking down of God's plan and purposes, and most definitely after causing havoc for those in leadership positions. Any time a person in a church undermines the authority of that church, they are under the operation of a python spirit.

Whether or not the person in authority is right as you perceive it to be, the active undermining of that person's authority is sabotage. If we disagree, there are scriptural ways of handling every situation. First of all, a loving response would be to pray and seek the wisdom of God.

Romans 13 speaks of submission to higher powers in the world system. "Wherefore ye must needs be subject, not only for wrath, but also for conscience sake" (Romans 13:5). The second and third chapters of 1 Peter

also speak of submission to authority. These are principles given by God so that we do not have rebellion
and anarchy.

If you feel that there are changes needed in leadership, you don't "pray them out." That amounts to nothing but "white" witchcraft. Using the anointing and the
Word of God for your own selfish desires against someone else's will is "white" witchcraft. Praying someone
out of their position is not God inspired.

Praying for God's will to be accomplished in their
lives is righteous. If a situation is not favorable in your
sight, pray in the Holy Ghost (unknown tongues), and
let Him deal with the situation while you walk in love.
As you earnestly pray, God will be faithful to give you
wisdom for every situation. Don't let yourself be
deceived and allow the spirit of python to manipulate
you.

Frequently the question is asked, "What do you do
when someone comes into the church, and is just a continuous troublemaker?" The person may even come to
you with words like these: "I am your prophet. I have
been sent to your church to be your prophet." You may
have never seen or heard about them before.

This may be a more obvious example, but it is
witchcraft. Many times these same people have been
wandering from church to church, and have proclaimed
themselves to be their prophet as well. They will come
into the church uninvited and have a word of the Lord
for the whole congregation, and most certainly have one
for the pastor. They will tell you everything that you
should be doing, and give you the entire plan that you
have been seeking to get from God for years.

What are you going to do with such an individual?
Along with corrective counseling, church leaders must

diligently pray. The false ones won't be able to stay under the pressure of prayer and the Word. Like a cancer cell that is not cooperating with healthy cells, these people need to change, or be cut out to avoid infecting healthy cells.

Diversionary Tactics

One of the strategies that is used by the spirit of python with great frequency, is that of diversionary tactics. If the enemy can keep you preoccupied in one area, he has an opening into another. While you are putting out brush fires here and there, he is covering up the real source of the problem. This is when you need to trust the Holy Spirit for the gift of discerning of spirits to be in operation.

When the young woman was following Paul and Silas around for days, she was not silent. In fact, she was crying out, calling much attention to herself, and taking attention away from the purpose of God at hand.

Anyone that has to always be the center of undivided attention is manipulating and controlling those giving the attention. They are being influenced by a spirit of python. If it is not dealt with according to the Word of God, there will be factions brewing, and a church split is not far behind. People will become deceived and seduced. Unless this ruling spirit is overcome, it will happen again and again.

Some churches are experiencing jealousy, strife, and competitive spirits, without real communion or fellowship among the brethren. You try to get people together, but it seems that you can't get the support you need. You know doing it is right, so you wind up doing it alone. All of this is python at work.

Confusion

Confusion in individuals is another outcome of python at work. It seems as if your mind is in a vise and you can't seem to organize your thinking or make a decision with peace. Confusion is a state of bewilderment, where your thinking is tumultuous. There is an undercurrent of unrest at work. First Corinthians 14:33 says, "For God is not the author of confusion, but of peace, as in all churches of the saints."

God's ways are always peace producing for the righteous. Romans 14:17 says, "For the kingdom of God is not meat and drink; but righteousness, and peace, and joy in the Holy Ghost." Jesus prayed to the Father and promised another Comforter. "And I will pray the Father, and he shall give you another Comforter..." (John 14:16).

There was no comfort in having this girl following Paul and Silas around, crying out and confusing the people. How could they, being Jews, known to have been worshippers of one Most High God, be in league with a cult worshipper of Apollo Pythius in the context of a multi-god mythological religion? You can see the contradiction immediately, and to be sure it was confusing to the Macedonians.

The apostle Paul was grieved in his spirit because there was every evil work trying to take place under the influence of this spirit of python. Romans 14:17 describes the kingdom of God as being "...righteousness, and peace, and joy in the Holy Ghost." None of these things were present, therefore, she was not of the kingdom of God.

Exalting Man Instead of God

She cried out that Paul and Silas were servants of the Most High God. That was true but there was something very wrong with it. Paul did not need to have a shill, a pitchman to lure onlookers, to do the work of the Lord.

Paul and Silas were not great men because they were servants of the Most High God. They were great men because the Most High God was exalted and they were humbled. Neither Paul, nor Silas, could be or do anything without the power of the Holy Spirit in manifestation. She was diverting attention away from the Most High God onto the servants. Python draws attention away from God and onto human beings.

There are times when I have been just about to minister the Word of God, when somebody begins to "prophesy" great and mighty things that I am going to do in the service. It is diverting attention away from God.

I can't do anything unless God does it through me. Ministers are deceived if they allow themselves to be puffed up in pride thinking that they are great. God is the only One Who is great, and mortals are privileged to have Him work through them.

She was really saying, "Follow Paul and Silas, and their glory." Following and glorifying man will always lead to destruction. Are we following a personality or the anointing? Following a personality will disappoint you somewhere down the road. The personality may even be very charismatic, but only the anointing will destroy the yoke of bondage.

In stark contrast to the nameless witch that followed Paul and Silas, is Lydia in Acts 16:14.

ACTS 16:14

14 And a certain woman named Lydia, a seller of purple, of the city of Thyatira, which worshipped God, heard us: whose heart the Lord opened, that she attended unto the things which were spoken of Paul.

Lydia was a willing and open listener to what Paul was ministering. There are people to whom you can talk, preach, teach, plead, and counsel, yet it all falls on seemingly deaf ears. Their hearts are simply not open to receive. We need to pray that the Lord opens their hearts like He opened Lydia's.

How are the two women of Acts 16 different? Lydia worshipped God before Paul ever showed up. The other wanted people to worship Paul. She wanted to worship humanity, and open the hearts of the people. Lydia heard the message of God because she first worshipped Him, and He was the One Who opened her heart. Lydia was not impressed by a personality. She received the words of the gospel of Jesus Christ.

Worshipping God seven days a week, not only on Sunday morning, is a major key to experiencing the glory and having an open heart to hear what the Spirit of the Lord wants to say. Lydia worshipped Him, and He was faithful to send a servant to reveal more of Himself.

Following after a man can be compared to Balaam and his donkey. The donkey spoke, but Balaam didn't get off the animal and follow after it. Surely we have at least that much wisdom. We should not confuse the vessel with the treasure. We need to be like the Bereans in Acts 17:11.

ACTS 17:11

11 These were more noble than those in Thessalonica, in that they received the word with all readiness of mind, and searched the scriptures daily, whether those things were so.

Many people are being tossed to and fro because they have taken another man's revelation without checking the Word of God. It could even be a good revelation, but if it is just added to your mental library as another piece of information, it is only another wind of doctrine for you.

When a new book comes out, or someone on television says a particular revelation is not correct, you won't know if it is or isn't, if you are just relying on hearsay evidence. If, on the other hand, you take a man's revelation, check it out with the Word of God, and in prayer seek the Holy Spirit about it, you will be convinced either one way or another.

Then, if someone denounces it, you won't be tossed about. It has then become your revelation, and the man who first spoke about it doesn't matter any more. You will have God's Word on the matter. If you speak in tongues, speaking in tongues being for today becomes your revelation. It is not a Pentecostal or Charismatic revelation, it has become yours, and nobody can take it away.

Revelations are going to flow, both pure and impure. For us to know for sure that they are of God, we have to take them to prayer, and the Word of God. When it becomes our revelation, we will not stumble over it, or fall away because of it. As an example, people could burn me at the stake and tell me speaking in an unknown tongue by the Holy Spirit is of the devil, and I would still continue to speak in tongues. I am that convinced of it because it is the revelation of Almighty God and a vital part of my lifestyle.

Grief

When a spirit of python is in operation, you will find a heaviness, sorrow, depression, and oppression hovering. Paul was grieved for many days. These things don't give up on their own. It is somewhat encouraging to us to note that Paul didn't get the answer right away. It took him a few days to discern what was happening. We may not catch on right away either.

Being grieved in the Spirit is described in Hebrews 5:14. "But strong meat belongeth to them that are of full age, even those who by reason of use have their SENSES EXERCISED TO DISCERN BOTH GOOD AND EVIL."

When something just doesn't seem right, yet all the outward evidence is contrary, this discernment of good and evil is working. Sometimes we even chastise ourselves for thinking suspiciously about people, when everything seems to say they are just wonderful.

I have seen immature people set into positions of leadership, even though they were not anointed for that time and place. Everything seemed right on the surface, but something inside was waving red flags. They might have even been wonderful in many ways, but not right for that position. The red flags waving was the voice of the Holy Spirit trying to warn that this was not right.

Unless something intervenes, there is certain to be a problem somewhere down the road. Something will happen to cause disillusionment, disappointment, or discouragement. When we don't obey the voice of the Holy Spirit, it ends up being a nasty predicament.

We need to test the spirits, and trust our own spirit. If you have been in this situation on either end, God is still big enough to restore everyone involved in His great forgiveness, so that everyone can move on with God.

Paul took control of his situation. He spoke to the spirit (notice not the woman), and said, "...I command thee in the name of Jesus Christ to come out of her...." (Acts 16:18a). He didn't engage in a conversation, or politely ask the demonic spirits to leave, or even ask God to make them leave. You must command them in the Name of Jesus.

Manipulative Spirits

In Acts 16:19, we find that the girl was not alone in her divination activities. She had masters over her that were profiting from her supernatural ability. They immediately saw that their source of income was gone when the spirit was cast out of her. They could no longer control or manipulate the girl, so they went after Paul and Silas for revenge.

✓ There is always manipulation involved with the spirit of divination. People under its influence are not open to correction. They always want to have things their way, and try to control every situation.

This is the hallmark of every cult and occult group. Freedom and liberty to pursue God is squashed. Individual and personal relationship with the Lord is negated, and usually there is a person or "guru" that acts as the mediary between you and spiritual growth. Personal decision making is virtually denied. You become dependent on the group or leader for your existence. Python's control is pervasive.

We see as Paul and Silas are brought before the rulers of the city, that this spirit will use whatever means it can to stop the spread of the gospel. It will find loopholes in laws, and it will even see to it that laws are changed, making it unlawful to even speak the Word of God. We have seen this in action in our own land.

The charges against Paul were, that he was troubling their city by teaching customs that were unlawful for them to observe. First of all, Paul never taught customs, he only taught about Jesus in the power of the Holy Spirit, and what he taught was even new to the Jews in that area. You can't have laws about something that never existed before. Paul ran into the same thing in Thessalonica as is described in Acts 17:5-8.

ACTS 17:5-8

5 But the Jews which believed not, moved with envy, took unto them certain lewd fellows of the baser sort, and gathered a company, and set all the city on an uproar, and assaulted the house of Jason, and sought to bring them out to the people.

6 And when they found them not, they drew Jason and certain brethren unto the rulers of the city, crying, These that have turned the world upside down are come hither also;

7 Whom Jason hath received: and these all do contrary to the decrees of Caesar, saying that there is another king, one Jesus.

8 And they troubled the people and the rulers of the city, when they heard these things.

✓ Python is very territorial. He does not want believers to take a city or a nation. He will fight viciously, and use every means possible to prevent a work of God from succeeding.

These people of Philippi had only customs and traditions and therefore, were resistant to the power of God unto salvation. Acts 16:22 says, "And the multitude rose up together against them...." They had a group mentality steeped in tradition. They may not even have known as individuals, what the charges were all about. This group mentality is evident even today when you see mass rallies against wholesome principles.

Paul and Silas had their clothing torn, had been beaten with a whip, and were thrown into a dungeon in chains. They knew what suffering for Christ was all about. Did they complain to the Lord or grumble? Acts 16:22-32 reveals that they turned to God in prayer, praise, and worship, and God's power was demonstrated.

✳ You might feel like you have been imprisoned, and there is no hope. As you pray, praise, and worship God, His power will be demonstrated in your life. Python can be removed in all circumstances by the power of the blood and the Name of Jesus, and by our obedience to God and His Word.

Sharing and Rejoicing

There was great sharing and rejoicing with the jailer and his household in that situation.

ACTS 16:32,34

32 And they spake unto him the word of the Lord, and to all that were in his house.

34 And when he had brought them into his house, he set meat before them, and rejoiced, believing in God with all his house.

✓ When python is working, you will find that people in the congregation are not sharing with one another. There is no real communion and fellowship. Conversely, there will be isolation, cliques, and special interest groups. There's an "every man for himself" attitude.

Caring, Sharing, and Rejoicing

Returning from one of my ministry trips in California, I was standing beside a porter with all of my baggage. I had a large purse and was searching around its many contents to get his tip. He said, "You don't have anything in there for a headache, do you?"

The anointing of God was still on me. I looked up into his eyes and said, "I don't have anything in this purse for a headache, but what I have I give to you. In the Name of Jesus, I command the source of that headache to be gone, and every bit of that pain to depart from your head now."

His eyes opened wide as I prayed for him. Then he looked at me with tears welling up, and said, "Well, I feel better already." Then he continued to say, "You know, you can tell. You should have seen the group that came through here today. We get them all the time. They had some wild thing on their jackets about God, an unholy mess. You should have seen the skycaps run from that group. Nobody wanted to take their luggage. They came through here grinning, but when you look into their eyes, you can just tell what they are."

As they say in Georgia, you can *grin like a horse eating briars*, it doesn't matter if it isn't coming from a pure heart. Do you suffer when another suffers? Do you rejoice when another is honored? That is the real test. When python is working, there is no sharing or rejoicing.

First Samuel 30 and 1 Samuel 22 tell of what happened to David at Ziklag. He transformed a bunch of distressed, disillusioned, discontented, indebted rejects into a mighty army for Israel. As long as he was the captain leading his army into victory, they were proud of him and telling of his greatness. Then while David and his men were away at a battle, the Amalekites made off with their wives, children and goods.

These same men who cheered him, now jeered him and were ready to stone him because they believed they were defeated. What did David do? He "...encouraged himself in the Lord his God" (1 Samuel 30:6). When the situation looks bad, wait on and rejoice in the Lord your God, and watch Him move on your behalf.

Paul at Ephesus

Paul's experience in Philippi was repeated in Ephesus.

ACTS 19:24-27

24 For a certain man named Demetrius, a silversmith, which made silver shrines for Diana, brought no small gain unto the craftsmen;

25 Whom he called together with the workmen of like occupation, and said, Sirs, ye know that by this craft we have our wealth.

26 Moreover ye see and hear, that not alone at Ephesus, but almost throughout all Asia, this Paul hath persuaded and turned away much people, saying that they be no gods, which are made with hands:

27 So that not only this our craft is in danger to be set at nought; but also that the temple of the great goddess Diana should be despised, and her magnificence should be destroyed, whom all Asia and the world worshippeth.

Here again we find that Demetrius perceived that his source of finances was threatened by the preaching of the gospel. With python in operation, the love of money and the fear of loss is always at the root.

Demetrius had such little vision or confidence in his craftsmanship that he could not see beyond idol-making as the source of his income. His craftsmanship could have very easily been used in making something besides idols. Had he received the gospel, God was more than able to have given him a whole new line of merchandise to produce, which could have been far more lucrative than what his idols produced. Python chokes visions and creativity.

Demetrius also bought the lie that the whole world worshipped Diana. This truly was ignorance. However, it is this kind of sweeping generalization that gets a crowd all stirred up to behave like a mob instead of a civilized group.

No doubt there were large numbers of people in Ephesus devoted to Diana, and Demetrius was able to incite the people based on their fundamental belief system. The great temple to this mythological deity was in Ephesus, and there was a large silversmith industry that centered around making shrines and idols to Diana. It is interesting to note that in their mythology, Diana was the twin sister of Apollo. It was the Apollo worshippers that gave Paul a difficult time in Philippi. The same spirit was at work in both cities.

Even if a belief system is widespread, such as the worship of Diana, it does not give credence to that belief merely because large numbers of people believe it. Cults are a worldwide phenomenon, but that does not make them right. God's Word is still the truth.

Because python was in control of the people, they were easily agitated, prideful and highly defensive. Acts 19:28 says, "And when they heard these sayings, they were full of wrath, and cried out, saying, Great is Diana of the Ephesians." Sudden anger that flares up is a sure indicator that demonic spirits are at work. It is the opposite of the fruit of the Holy Spirit.

It is amazing how nervous spirits get when they are in the presence of those filled with the Holy Spirit.

ACTS 19:32

32 Some therefore cried one thing, and some another: for the assembly was confused; and the more part knew not wherefore they were come together.

It simply says that they were so befuddled that most of them didn't even know why they gathered together. That ruling spirit was manipulating and controlling them to the point where they didn't know what they were doing.

Disguises

I SAMUEL 28:5-8

5 And when Saul saw the host of the Philistines, he was afraid, and his heart greatly trembled.

6 And when Saul inquired of the Lord, the Lord answered him not, neither by dreams, nor by Urim, nor by prophets.

7 Then said Saul unto his servants, Seek me a woman that hath a familiar spirit, that I may go to her, and inquire of her. And his servants said to him, Behold, there is a woman that hath a familiar spirit at Endor.

8 And Saul disguised himself, and put on other raiment, and he went, and two men with him, and they came to the woman by night: and he said, I pray thee, divine unto me by the familiar spirit, and bring me him up, whom I shall name unto thee.

Saul gathered his army in Gilboa and saw the enormity of the Philistine army in Shunem. He was extraordinarily fearful as he went to the Lord for wisdom. Perhaps because of his great fear, he was unable to hear the Word of the Lord. God does not respond to fear. He responds to faith.

Verses five through seven speak of Saul's character and lack of fellowship with God. Saul had no conscience about seeking out someone who operated in demonic methods, as soon as he didn't hear from God in the manner to which he was accustomed. Saul knew that it was an abomination to God to seek out a witch for wisdom. It was Saul who outlawed witchcraft, yet he was carried away with his own desires, and lack of trust in God.

Saul went to the witch of Endor by his own will, in spite of knowing better. It was direct participation on his part. The human will is our strongest attribute. By the exercise of our will, we either receive or reject salvation. Likewise, deceiving spirits manipulate the human will to get it to submit.

Instead of trusting God and seeking Him with a pure heart, Saul relied on the world's alternative to spirituality. Deceit had gripped his judgment and divination was the choice that came out of his soul.

Verse eight says that Saul disguised himself when he went to see the witch. He did not want to be recognized by her or any others. He exchanged his kingly robes, representing authority and rule, for something far less.

We also have kingly raiment. They include the robe of righteousness, the garments of praise and holiness, and the mantle of service. Deceiving spirits want you to remove your kingly garments for common clothes and submit yourself to their control. They also try to deceive you into desiring another person's mantle instead of wearing your own.

Many churches are suffering because their leaders claim to be pastors, prophets, apostles, evangelists, or teachers, when they are not called to walk in that ministry gift. A minister who is not walking in his calling is a most miserable person. Some are not called to be a five-fold minister. Total satisfaction comes when you are being productive in the call of God on your life, whatever that may be.

Saul stepped out of his mantle, and stooped down to a wicked woman to give him direction because he was not hearing from God. The irony is that God does not withhold any good thing from those who love Him. It was Saul who was withholding his heart, confidence, and fidelity from God. God does not reveal His Will for you to consider, but rather for you to unconditionally obey. Anything else will end in disaster.

1 CHRONICLES 10:13,14

13 So Saul died for his transgression which he committed against the Lord, even against the word of the Lord, which he kept not, and also for asking counsel of one that had a familiar spirit, to inquire of it;

14 And inquired not of the Lord: therefore he slew him, and turned the kingdom unto David the son of Jesse.

Ultimately, he lost everything. He lost his fellowship with God by not seeking God's direction, and then he lost his life for his transgression. In addition, his descendants also lost their royal lineage.

It is also noteworthy that in verses thirteen and fourteen, the word "Lord" is used. This indicated the covenant name Jehovah. Saul broke his covenant with God by seeking out supernatural wisdom from another source.

Saul was a man chosen by God. He was in covenant with God, and the mantle of leadership of Israel was upon him.

1 SAMUEL 9:16

16 Tomorrow about this time I will send thee a man out of the land of Benjamin, and thou shalt anoint him to be captain over my people Israel, that he may save my people out of the hand of the Philistines: for I have looked upon my people, because their cry is come unto me.

Saul was anointed to be the captain of his people to save them from the Philistines. He remained a strong leader as long as he was obedient to the voice of God. When he ceased to seek the Lord for wisdom, he removed the mantle of leadership from himself, and with it God's protection.

A strong principle that the Lord gave me many years ago was, "If you cannot hear My Word and My Will for yourself, how do you think you can get yourself in a position to hear My Word for My people?"

Besides the obvious spirit of divination (python) directly being sought by Saul, there is the fact that Saul disguised himself and went to the witch under cover of night. Deceit and pretense are the puppet strings that make the operation of python work.

When Saul removed his kingly mantle, he laid aside his authority and office. He put on pretense to hide

50

what he knew was a wrong action, that is, seeking familiar spirits. He would never have been deceived if he had walked in his mantle of authority. By exchanging his raiment of authority for one of pretense, he lowered himself and lost the respect, rights, and privileges of his position.

This is one reason some churches fall apart. Different people are wearing the wrong mantle. They remove their own, thinking someone else's is more desirable. When they tried to put Saul's armor on David, he refused to wear it saying that it didn't fit.

The wrong fit was more than just physical. David knew that as long as Saul was alive, his position and anointing as king must not be violated. David respected Saul's office and refused to take the throne away from him.

God has a mantle for every human being in the body of Christ. Therein is the protection to do what He has called each of us to do. Therein is the authority, anointing, gift, and ability to carry out the call.

Seeking Familiar Spirits

By calling on familiar spirits for wisdom and guidance, Saul signed his own death warrant. Whereas life can only produce life, death can only produce death. This is the ultimate victory for python.

1 CHRONICLES 10:13,14

13 So Saul died for his transgression which he committed against the Lord, even against the word of the Lord, which he kept not, and also for asking counsel of one that had a familiar spirit, to inquire of it;

14 And inquired not of the Lord: therefore he slew him, and turned the kingdom unto David the son of Jesse.

Divination, or operating by the spirit of python, is a transgression against the Lord. The Lord is a covenant keeping God. Therefore, divination is breaking covenant with God.

✱   You will find that when the spirit of python is attacking a church, people will be unable to sustain commitment to each other, the leadership, or the church. The pastor has certain rights, respect, and privileges entitled to him by virtue of his position as a leader. Along with this comes the great responsibilities of leadership. When python is in action, python wants to be in control, rather than the rightful leader.

Fear Tactics

Saul was anointed to save his people from the Philistines. He was supposed to lead them, rule wisely over them, and keep his mantle. When he went to see the witch, he was operating in fear. When faith in God is absent, the only force that can operate is fear and fear empowers the spirit of python to operate.

When the devil is setting a trap, fear will bait you into it. People will begin to wonder, and ask themselves, "Am I supposed to be doing this? Did I miss God? Should I be selling cars instead of pastoring?" Now, there is nothing wrong with selling cars if that is what God wants you to do. However, if He wants you to be a pastor, you can be sure you will be miserable doing anything else.

As in Saul's case, the enemy will use fear as the front line weapon. Fear about whether or not things will work out, fear about provision, fear about what others will think of you or what you are going to do. These are the kinds of fears that will try to take root. You may be tempted to back down from God's Word and His Will. You may even be tempted to give up.

2 TIMOTHY 1:6,7

6 Wherefore I put thee in remembrance that thou stir up the gift of God, which is in thee by the putting on of my hands.

7 For God hath not given us the spirit of fear; but of power, and of love, and of a sound mind.

It is of primary importance to eliminate fear. In Gideon's army, the fearful ones were sent home first. One fearful man will infect an entire army. The ten fearful spies transferred their fears to an entire nation and kept them in the wilderness for 40 years (Numbers 13 and 14). Motivated by fear, Saul sought a witch for direction.

DEUTERONOMY 20:1

1 When thou goest out to battle against thine enemies, and seest horses, and chariots, and a people more than thou, be not afraid of them: for the Lord thy God is with thee, which brought thee up out of the land of Egypt.

In this chapter, God reveals what He will not allow in His army. Weakness of heart and spirit is not permitted. You have to send the weak home, because one fearful person will infect the whole army with fear.

Python will cause the people to become fearful, weak, and weary. They will begin to question their call, their position, and their vision. This is python at work trying to squeeze you out of what God has called you to do and be.

The opposite is 2 Timothy 1:6,7, which says, "Wherefore I put thee in remembrance that thou stir up the gift of God, which is in thee by the putting on of my hands. For God hath not given us the spirit of fear; but of power, and of love, and of a sound mind." In other words, encourage yourself in the Lord, release that boldness, sound mind, power, and love that is in your spirit.

✓ When Saul didn't hear from God right away, he sought a diviner. Assuming you have bound the enemy, you must learn that when God doesn't seem to speak, just stay put, fixed on the faith that God is working on your behalf. Don't seek flesh and blood, but rather, get the vision from God and go with it.

✓ If you are contemplating doing something and you have doubts, don't do it because it is not by faith. Romans 14:23b says, "...for whatsoever is not of faith is sin." If there is a check inside that you shouldn't do it, listen to it. That is how you learn to operate in the Spirit. This is not the fear of flesh, but the check deep down inside in your spirit.

For example, suppose you believe that you should give someone a telephone call because of their need. You might even think that you have a special word of encouragement from the Lord for them, yet you know deep inside that person is not even going to be home when you call. What should you do? Just get on your face, and pray it through. You don't even need to let them know that you had a word for them. Pray and let the Holy Spirit be in control.

Chapter 3
Idolatry and the Ruling Spirit

LEVITICUS 18:25
25 And the land is defiled: therefore I do visit the iniquity thereof upon it, and the land itself vomiteth out her inhabitants.

Long before settlers came to this land, and eventually began to expand its borders, there were several nations of people, native Americans, who inhabited the territories for an undeterminable number of centuries. Not much has remained to document the ancient history of these people, but there does remain the knowledge of their ways over the recent centuries. Their heritage is rich and as valuable as those of other nations.

The record shows that they have been victims of great atrocities, as well as perpetrators of some. Be that as it may, there is an issue that we cannot escape. When idolatry is practiced by *any* people, group, or nation, their land is defiled, and at some point they will experience violent dispossession.

It is a matter of historical fact, that native American nations across the whole scope of this land, worshipped idols of nature gods. Some of their descendants still do to this day.

Early European settlers also brought along with them religious and traditional baggage, making God's Word of no effect. Later waves of immigration from every part of the earth added to the patchwork called America. Each ethnic and national group has added rich culture to the fabric of our nation, but the negative side has been added as well. The land has been defiled.

Curses need to be broken by the power of the blood and Name of Jesus. In 1980, prayer went forth to break the curse over our Presidents elected to office in a year ending with zero. The story follows, that a *shamman* (a Native American prophet, healer, and religious leader), pronounced that curse because of a treaty broken by one of our early Presidents.

Since then, every President elected in a year ending with zero has died in office. President Kennedy, elected in 1960, was the last President to die in office. There was a serious assassination attempt on President Reagan, but was obviously unsuccessful. Even before he was elected, prayer went forth to break this curse.

At an Intercessors' 500 meeting, one of the speakers who had been in the ministry for thirty-five years and by no means a novice, shared that her church had been praying and fasting for forty days. Each church member participated in some way, fasting one meal, fasting one day a week, or in whatever way they could take part in prayer and fasting.

They were having difficulty in taking their city for Jesus, but during the prayer and fasting, the Lord revealed to them that the difficulty was a result of worship to idols on the high hills of that area by its original inhabitants. The land was defiled and cursed. The church congregation went up to those high hills, broke those curses, and decreed God's Word over the area. They got results.

In 1978, I saw by the Spirit a particular church, even though I had not yet been there. At that time, I saw demons seated in a specific location in the church. When I ministered there in 1984, I spoke to the pastor and he verified that the 1978 leadership of the church was seated exactly where I had seen those demons six years before. I prophesied that the foundation of that work was built over a curse, only to find out later that a well known prophetess of Satan owned that property before them.

Fifty years prior, the founding pastor had a vision for a mighty supernatural work of God, yet the church experienced split after split. When I ministered there in 1984, the current pastor was ready to throw in the towel. He wanted to give the church over to an associate pastor, thinking, "Maybe my time is up and I'm finished." As it turned out, the associate pastor later left, along with several people.

I had prophesied that there would be an "Aaron and Hur" who would move into the situation to support the pastor and uphold his arms during this future time of unrest. That word came to pass. God sent the "Aaron and Hur" that he needed.

In addition to those two men, the Lord led a younger pastoral couple to unite their church with this church to work together. They broke the curse over that property and God is using these two congregations that united, to continue the work in fulfilling the founding pastor's vision. God's plan is for that church to be a lighthouse to the government and a positive influence in the area.

God warned the Israelites, that as they possessed the land, they were to refrain from the sinful practices of idolatry.

DEUTERONOMY 12:29-32

29 When the Lord thy God shall cut off the nations from before thee, whither thou goest to possess them, and thou succeedest them, and dwellest in their land;

30 Take heed to thyself that thou be not snared by following them, after that they be destroyed from before thee; and that thou inquire not after their gods, saying, How did these nations serve their gods? even so will I do likewise.

31 Thou shalt not do so unto the Lord thy God: for every abomination to the Lord, which he hateth, have they done unto their gods; for even their sons and their daughters they have burnt in the fire to their gods.

32 What thing soever I command you, observe to do it: thou shalt not add thereto, nor diminish from it.

Being curious about idolatrous worship is a snare. We know from the history of Israel, that when the tribes of Israel engaged in marrying idol worshippers and permitted idolatry to be practiced in their land, destruction always followed. The land became defiled. When they repented, they were restored.

Frequently people are not aware of the historical significance of their land. They just don't know of any past idolatrous practices or curses that may have defiled their land. Some people have difficulty selling their land because the land is defiled and the spirit of python is in operation.

What can you do if there is a possibility of your land being defiled? The prophets said, "Hear, Oh land." Speak to the land and command it to come into your possession. Take some of that earth into your hands and speak out and say, "All defilement and curses are broken and this land is purified by the finished work of Calvary. You are redeemed from the curse in the Name of Jesus."

The blood of the Lord Jesus Christ was spilled upon the earth for its redemption as God's people take it by faith. Call that land into your hands as your possession out of the hand of curses, and out of the hands of foreign gods. If you are trying to sell it, command the land that belongs to you to be sold. When you are finished, throw the soil to the wind and praise God. He will do what needs to be done.

Rebellion and Witchcraft

Under the Old Covenant, God did not permit witches to live. "Thou shalt not suffer a witch to live" (Exodus 22:18). That may seem like strong consequences, but the pervasive influence of witchcraft can destroy a nation.

1 SAMUEL 15:22-24

22 And Samuel said, Hath the Lord as great delight in burnt offerings and sacrifices, as in obeying the voice of the Lord? Behold, to obey is better than sacrifice, and to hearken than the fat of rams.

23 For rebellion is as the sin of witchcraft, and stubbornness is as iniquity and idolatry. Because thou hast rejected the word of the Lord, he hath also rejected thee from being king.

24 And Saul said unto Samuel, I have sinned: for I have transgressed the commandment of the Lord, and thy words: because I feared the people, and obeyed their voice.

In verse 23, witchcraft is clearly identified as a sin, and compared in similitude with rebellion. If those who practiced witchcraft deserved death, then those who practiced rebellion deserved like punishment since the two practices were equated. Before we write it off as Old Covenant law, and not applicable to our lives, what principle in this response to witchcraft transcends the law?

There are those who would want to cast out rebellion when they encounter it in the church. Like witchcraft, it cannot be cast out, it has to die. It is a work of the flesh influenced by demonic forces. It simply must be put to death because it is in total opposition to the fruit of the Spirit.

GALATIANS 5:17

17 For the flesh lusteth against the Spirit, and the Spirit against the flesh: and these are contrary the one to the other: so that ye cannot do the things that ye would.

Witchcraft and rebellion are manifested works of the flesh that have no part in the kingdom of God.

The root of rebellion is fear of the people, and obeying them instead of God. Leaders in the body of Christ cannot be as Saul was in fearing the people. In so doing, he lost his position as king.

Church leaders today risk losing their positions of leadership when they yield to fear of the congregation. The church will begin to deteriorate with strife and divisions, and sooner or later, the leaders are no longer doing what God called them to do. Unless they change, their end will be as Saul's, without a kingdom. Only when leaders hear and obey God will they find their way successful.

Zechariah 10:2

2 For the idols have spoken vanity, and the diviners have seen a lie, and have told false dreams; they comfort in vain: therefore they went their way as a flock, they were troubled, because there was no shepherd.

There are those who are without a local pastor. In some cases, there are those who refuse to submit to a local pastor. A God-ordained and God-obedient pastor is a protective covering for the sheep. Without such a pastor, a sheep is open season for seducing spirits. God gave the local church and pastor for our safety and protection.

Following Vanities

2 KINGS 17:14,15

14 Notwithstanding they would not hear, but hardened their necks, like to the neck of their fathers, that did not believe in the Lord their God.

15 And they rejected his statutes, and his covenant that he made with their fathers, and his testimonies which he testified against them; and they followed vanity, and became vain, and went after the heathen that were round about them, concerning whom the Lord had charged them, that they should not do like them.

Because of their hard attitudes and unwillingness to obey God, the Northern Kingdom of Israel fell into idolatry, witchcraft, rebellion, and every evil thing. They followed vanities which led them to do unthinkable evil deeds. As a result, their kingdom was utterly devastated. They were dispersed and cut off from their heritage. The spirit of python has no mercy. Where he is allowed to work, he will strangle every last spark of life.

When people become stiff-necked and hard-hearted, python is working. This is the fruit of his hand. When people are under this kind of influence, including fervent believers, they just won't listen to anybody.

I have seen the enemy influence intercessors to shut themselves away for inordinate lengths of time of prayer with the intent of purifying themselves. There is a time for being alone with God and it is without question, the most important aspect of our walk with the Lord. However, when it gets out of balance and a person gets into extremes, you know that it's not God.

They will tell you, "I've got to purify myself. God is calling me into the prayer closet to pray and be alone with Him to purify myself." If that is true, why was the blood of Jesus shed? His blood continually cleanses us from all unrighteousness, and it is not an act of work on our part, but grace and mercy from God. The secret place of the Most High God has far greater dynamics than any self-purification. In fact, the two cannot be compared to each other.

You may call them six months later and they're still isolated and cut off from the mainstream of Christian life. Their marriage intimacy is gone, fellowship and communion with the saints is non-existent, and their whole perspective becomes warped. They perceive everyone as unholy, and cast a cynical eye of judgment on everything. They don't enjoy anything or anyone, including themselves.

When you try to talk to them, not only do they turn a deaf ear, but they tell you that you are unholy and need to be purged. Because you don't accept their counsel, they decide that your relationship with them is unholy and needs to be ended. It would be a comedy if it weren't so pathetic. It denies the authority and power of Jesus as well as the meaning of His death and resurrection.

When you know something is wrong, confess it, and command it to leave by the power of the Name and blood of Jesus. Then leave the prayer closet charged with the power of the Holy Spirit and do something for God.

False Prophecy

Because of lying vanities, and the need to maintain a front before the people, false prophets of the past and present have said all manner of false things that have created havoc. It is because divination is at work instead of the Holy Spirit giving prophecy.

MICAH 3:5-7

5 Thus saith the Lord concerning the prophets that make my people err, that bite with their teeth, and cry, Peace; and he that putteth not into their mouths, they even prepare war against him.

6 Therefore night shall be unto you, that ye shall not have a vision; and it shall be dark unto you, that ye shall not divine; and the sun shall go down over the prophets, and the day shall be dark over them.

7 Then shall the seers be ashamed, and the diviners confounded: yea, they shall all cover their lips; for there is no answer of God.

This is what happens when python is permitted to work.

In contrast, Daniel 2:2-49 is an excellent example of how God operates. The magicians, astrologers, and sorcerers were powerless and were not able to tell the king his dream and its interpretation. Nebuchadnezzar was so infuriated that he ordered them all to be executed, including Daniel.

Daniel didn't even have the answer, but he had enough sense to know who did. He had to seek God, Who then gave him the interpretation of the king's dream. Because of Daniel's faithfulness and reliance on Almighty God, he was exalted in the kingdom. Revelation of truth comes from God alone.

Diviners, sorcerers, astrologers, and those of that ilk speak lying vanities that are profitless. When people are deceived, they don't realize that deception has them in its grip.

They say that they have heard from the Lord, when they really have not. False dreams and interpretations come forth. Their comfort is nothing more than a seducing spirit. Trouble follows them. Usually they are not submitted to or receiving care from a pastor.

False prophets were speaking boldly to the nation of Israel as is revealed in Jeremiah 27:14,15. The objective of lying spirits was to destroy them by their obedience to the voices of false prophecy.

JEREMIAH 27:14,15

14 Therefore hearken not unto the words of the prophets that speak unto you, saying, Ye shall not serve the king of Babylon: for they prophesy a lie unto you.

15 For I have not sent them, saith the Lord, yet they prophesy a lie in my name; that I might drive you out, and that ye might perish, ye, and the prophets that prophesy unto you.

Not only does this spirit of divination want to destroy the people, but it also wants to destroy the vessel it uses to bring about this devastation.

The consequences for falsely prophesying in Old Testament days were most severe. False prophets were put to death. The criteria was simple. If the prophecy did not come to pass, the prophet was executed.

In the New Covenant, we do not have that directive from the Lord, but we do have the responsibility of rightly judging the prophecy.

1 THESSALONIANS 5:19-21

19 Quench not the Spirit.

20 Despise not prophesyings.

21 Prove all things; hold fast that which is good.

When someone prophesies in the church, and it isn't quite right, God doesn't fall off His throne because one of His children made a mistake. There is a place for training, encouraging, and allowing people to grow in the gifts, without suppressing them.

However, there is also a place of discerning when python, divination, and the spirit of Jezebel is in action. They are the ones who prophesy a lie for the purpose of removing you from your land. In other words, they want to take your position in order that you be driven out and perish.

Python's Companions

Three spirits are often found working in conjunction with python. As with cockroaches, where you may find one, there is usually another lurking somewhere. One of them is a beguiling spirit, another is a seducing spirit, and the third is a Jezebel spirit.

Beguiling Spirit

The first place we find the beguiling spirit in action is in Genesis 3:4,5.

GENESIS 3:4,5

4 And the serpent said unto the woman, Ye shall not surely die:

5 For God doth know that in the day ye eat thereof, then your eyes shall be opened, and ye shall be as gods, knowing good and evil.

The evil spirit was saying that God lied when He told Adam and Eve that they would die if they ate of the tree of the knowledge of good and evil. In other words, through subtle suggestion, beguiling spirits try to get you to believe that God really doesn't mean what He says. In essence, it is a liar that calls God a liar.

In 2 Corinthians 11, Paul addresses the church at Corinth, and expresses a plea from his heart concerning their minds being influenced by a beguiling spirit.

2 CORINTHIANS 11:2,3

2 For I am jealous over you with godly jealousy: for I have espoused you to one husband, that I may present you as a chaste virgin to Christ.

3 But I fear, lest by any means, as the serpent beguiled Eve through his subtilty, so your minds should be corrupted from the simplicity that is in Christ.

Paul said that he espoused them to one husband to be a chaste virgin of Jesus Christ, and not seek after another.

Beguiling spirits try to pull you away from Jesus Christ and the leaders that God has placed over you. We are in covenant and need to stay where God has directed us, for as long as He decides that we need to be there. It is the beguiling spirits that entice people to drift from church to church. Each of us needs a local body. Pastors need to be cemented to the people, and the people to the pastors.

Subtle mind games are the specialty of this spirit. As in 2 Corinthians 11:3, it corrupts the simplicity that is in Christ. It wants to complicate things. You might have at some time walked away from a service hearing someone say, "That sure was deep stuff!" It was so deep, nobody knew what was said.

When the wisdom of Jesus speaks, it is so simple that you would have to work hard to miss it. Believers gets the message when Jesus gives it.

Seducing Spirits

Second Timothy 3:1-9 very carefully outlines the working of seducing spirits and tells what is at the root of the wickedness described in the fourth chapter of First Timothy. It admonishes us that there will be those "Having a form of godliness, but denying the power thereof..." (2 Timothy 3:5a).

Why do cultists, for example, present such a sweet image? What is their drawing power? They are operating under seducing spirits, which draws in those unaware, like honey draws flies. Unfortunately, when they get what they want, they are through with you. Seducing spirits always intend on destroying the victim.

MARK 13:22,23

22 For false Christs and false prophets shall rise, and shall shew signs and wonders, to seduce, if it were possible, even the elect.

23 But take ye heed: behold, I have foretold you all things.

In these scriptures, Jesus gives us a sobering warning to be on guard.

Paul also, under the inspiration of the Holy Spirit, strongly admonishes us to overcome seducing spirits by devotedly holding to sound doctrine.

2 TIMOTHY 3:13-17

13 But evil men and seducers shall wax worse and worse, deceiving, and being deceived.

14 But continue thou in the things which thou hast learned and hast been assured of, knowing of whom thou hast learned them;

15 And that from a child thou hast known the holy scriptures, which are able to make thee wise unto salvation through faith which is in Christ Jesus.

16 All scripture is given by inspiration of God, and is profitable for doctrine, for reproof, for correction, for instruction in righteousness:

17 That the man of God may be perfect, thoroughly furnished unto all good works.

Just as there were false prophets in Ezekiel's day, there are prophets today seducing the body of Christ. One of the most descriptive revelations of seducing false prophets is given in the 13th chapter of Ezekiel. It is just as applicable today as it was then.

EZEKIEL 13:1-5

1 And the word of the Lord came unto me, saying,

2 Son of man, prophesy against the prophets of Israel that prophesy, and say thou unto them that prophesy out of their own hearts, Hear ye the word of the Lord;

3 Thus saith the Lord God; Woe unto the foolish prophets, that follow their own spirit, and have seen nothing!

4 O Israel, thy prophets are like the foxes in the deserts.

5 Ye have not gone up into the gaps, neither made up the hedge for the house of Israel to stand in the battle in the day of the Lord.

✓ One of the chief characteristics of a false prophet who is under the influence of a seducing spirit, is that they don't pray. They don't seek God. They don't bridge the gap for the people that God sends to them for ministry.

True prophets are known more for prayer than prophecy. In James 5:17, for example, the focus is not Elias prophesying great words, but rather that he was a man of prayer to the degree that what he prayed for, came to pass. Prophets who don't pray get themselves and others into trouble.

Jezebel Spirit

1 KINGS 16:31

31 And it came to pass, as if it had been a light thing for him to walk in the sins of Jeroboam the son of Nebat, that he took to wife Jezebel the daughter of Ethbaal king of the Zidonians, and went and served Baal, and worshipped him.

King Ahab's problems in ruling his kingdom began with disobedience in marrying an idolatrous heathen. He was already known to be wicked, but he compounded his evil by marrying Jezebel. The spirit that controlled Jezebel always goes after leadership. It steals worship away from God, and replaces it with false worship.

It is easy to see how python, seducing spirits, beguiling spirits, and Jezebel spirits work together to bring about ruin. Jezebel, a zealous worshipper of Baal and Ashteroth from Sidon, brought the most vile forms of Canaanite idol worship to the Israelites.

In order to please her, King Ahab built her a worship center in Samaria, the capital city of the Northern

Kingdom of Israel. Her influence, more than any other single event, caused the downfall and utter devastation of the Northern Kingdom of Israel.

✓ When a Jezebel spirit is allowed to influence individuals in a local church, <u>false worship</u> will be evidenced, and ultimately the downfall of that church will come.

Jezebel had the true prophets of God terrorized. Obadiah hid one hundred of them in a cave, where they existed on bread and water. After Elijah slew the prophets of Baal, Jezebel was enraged and threatened to kill him.

1 KINGS 19:2

2 Then Jezebel sent a messenger unto Elijah, saying, So let the gods do to me, and more also, if I make not thy life as the life of one of them by to morrow about this time.

Little did she know that she cursed herself by the words of her own mouth.

This spirit operates in men as well as women. It doesn't necessarily desire a female body. King Ahab lusted after Naboth's vineyard, and when he was turned down, Jezebel said to him, "...Why is thy spirit so sad, that thou eatest no bread?" (1 Kings 21:5).

✓ When you are with someone carrying this spirit, <u>you feel drained</u>. Even if you're feeling great, a few minutes with this person makes you ready to take a rest. There is a melancholy around them, and it may even make you lose your appetite. For sure, it will cause you to lose your appetite for the things of God.

King Ahab tried to buy Naboth's vineyard, but Naboth wouldn't sell it to him. He even offered Naboth another vineyard to replace it. Naboth considered his land a sacred trust from God, and <u>chose to obey God</u> rather than the king.

Jezebel's response was typical of her character. She took charge of the situation. She said to Ahab, "...Dost thou now govern the kingdom of Israel?..." (1 Kings 21:7a). She was taunting him, challenging his authority as king.

Jesus was taunted by that same threat during his forty day fast in the desert of Judea. It is the same spirit that ridicules pastors and others, challenging their competence.

King Ahab, in his pitiful weakness, allowed her to take charge. Using King Ahab's name and authority, Jezebel wrote letters to the leaders of the city about Naboth. Applying King Ahab's royal seal to make it look official, she made it appear like he approved of the letters she wrote. Deception is always involved with this spirit.

✓ Those under the influence of the Jezebel spirit will use other people's names and act like they have been given approval for what they do. When a person is being used of God, he doesn't need anyone else's approval.

Jezebel's plot included providing false witnesses against Naboth and it resulted in his murder.

1 KINGS 21:13

13 And there came in two men, children of Belial, and sat before him: and the men of Belial witnessed against him, even against Naboth, in the presence of the people, saying, Naboth did blaspheme God and the king. Then they carried him forth out of the city, and stoned him with stones, that he died.

When Jezebel spirits are working, people speak lies in order to gain special favor or position. Included in this operation, there will be those that the devil raises up as accusers of the brethren. Naboth's vineyard was taken illegally and he was murdered. There was gross injustice, manipulation, and control. It caused the entire nation of Israel to sin.

1 KINGS 21:22

22 And will make thine house like the house of Jeroboam the son of Nebat, and like the house of Baasha the son of Ahijah, for the provocation wherewith thou hast provoked me to anger, and made Israel to sin.

Generation curses result in the operation of this spirit. In Ahab's case, Elijah proclaimed,

1 KINGS 21:29

29 Seest thou how Ahab humbleth himself before me? because he humbleth himself before me, I will not bring the evil in his days: but in his son's days will I bring the evil upon his house.

The Jezebel spirit will cause people to sell themselves to work evil. This includes all forms of prostitution and witchcraft and lies.

2 KINGS 17:17

17 And they caused their sons and their daughters to pass through the fire, and used divination and enchantments, and sold themselves to do evil in the sight of the Lord, to provoke him to anger.

2 KINGS 9:22b

22 ...What peace, so long as the whoredoms of thy mother Jezebel and her witchcrafts are so many?

Jezebel met her end just as was prophesied. As she was leaning out of a window ridiculing Jehu, some eunuchs threw her down. Jehu drove his chariot over her body, splattering her blood on the horses and palace wall. Before they could bury her, dogs ate her flesh. After those demons were finished with her, she was totally consumed.

Jezebel is spoken of in Revelation 2:18-20, referring to the church at Thyatira.

REVELATION 2:18-20

18 And unto the angel of the church in Thyatira write; These things saith the Son of God, who hath his eyes like unto a flame of fire, and his feet are like fine brass;

19 I know thy works, and charity, and service, and faith, and thy patience, and thy works; and the last to be more than the first.

✓ **20 Notwithstanding I have a few things against thee, because thou sufferest that woman Jezebel, which calleth herself a prophetess, to teach and to seduce my servants to commit fornication, and to eat things sacrificed unto idols.**

The spirit of Jezebel was found right in the church. The Thyatira church had everything going for it, works, love, service, and patience. They were to be commended for it. However, we see that the spirit of Jezebel was allowed entrance.

She may call herself a prophetess, that is, one who speaks for the Lord, but this spirit operates in men as well as women. It doesn't particularly desire a female body. The woman Jezebel is figuratively applied to a sect that caused great harm to the church at Thyatira.

Notice that the same symptoms are evident. False prophets that teach and seduce, fornication (Jezebel worshipped Ashteroth, the grotesque goddess of fertility), and eating things sacrificed to idols. All of these were in direct opposition to the decrees of the Jerusalem council in Acts 15:28,29. This same spirit of Jezebel led the false prophets in Thyatira.

✓ Revelation 2:21 says, "And I gave her space to repent of her fornication; and she repented not." You will find spiritual adultery wherever there is a Jezebel spirit. This spirit will divide the local body and cause its people to be disloyal to God, the church, and its leaders. Jezebel spirits question and challenge sound doctrine. The very depths of Satan go with this spirit.

God, however, is searching hearts for right attitudes, aims, motives, and purposes.

Recognizing Jezebel

Wherever python is the ruling spirit, Jezebel and her other two companions, the beguiling and seducing spirits are usually active to some degree. God will reveal to you what is in operation.

Someone once came to me and said, "Bobbie Jean, I think I'm under a Jezebel spirit. What do I do?"

I answered, "You get on your face and repent. Ask God to forgive you. Command it to leave you in the Name of the Lord Jesus Christ! Put it under the blood of the Lord Jesus Christ. Declare to God that you chose to be free of it. Declare to Him that it is not your will to serve Jezebel. Your will is to serve Him."

How are you able to tell if it is the work of flesh or the work of a demon? A work of the flesh is something you can control and have permanent victory. When a demon is involved, you get rest, but no matter how hard you try it is only temporary. It just seems that you fall into the same trap of depression, or lying, or manipulation, or whatever it may be. If you examine it carefully you will likely find it working in past generations.

If that spirit tries to visit you again, just proclaim, "You're not coming into this house. I am the house of the Lord. You get out in the Name of Jesus." Then continue to praise and worship God to maintain the victory in your life.

The spirits will get the message. The main idea that you need to fix in your mind is that "It is written..." is vital. We are not battling with flesh and blood. The Word of God has gone forth. Take it to prayer and remember, what you have gained by prayer, you must maintain by prayer and obedience to God and His Word.

Chapter 4
Opposition to God's Work

Whenever someone is being used by God to further the kingdom, opposition from the evil one rises up to try and stop the work. Studying the experience of Nehemiah will help to identify those elements that hinder God's plans from being carried through to fruition.

Nehemiah was the cupbearer to Artaxerxes, the Persian king who gave Nehemiah permission and supplies to go to Jerusalem to rebuild the walls and gates of the city. In Hebrew the word "cupbearer," which is transliterated *mashkeh*, literally means one giving a drink. In our society, it has little meaning. However, in its historical context, the cupbearer was a man of high position in the palace.

Treachery and assassination attempts were just as much a concern of world leaders in the ancient world as they are today. In this context, the cupbearer would be responsible for serving the king his wine, making certain it was not poisoned. However, his responsibilities went beyond wine tasting.

As cupbearer, he was a personal confidant and counselor to the king. He was also highly trusted in personal decisions as well as matters of state. Because of his close relationship to the king, he knew the desires and heart of the king. There was probably nothing about Artaxerxes that his cupbearer, Nehemiah, didn't know.

A report came to Nehemiah about the conditions of the Jews in Jerusalem. Reproach and affliction were upon them because of the broken down walls of the city and burned gates. In those days, the walls of the city and its gates were vital to its safety and protection from marauding tribes.

Nehemiah, being a prophet of God and an intercessor, wept, fasted, and prayed on behalf of his people.

NEHEMIAH 1:4-6

4 And it came to pass, when I heard these words, that I sat down and wept, and mourned certain days, and fasted, and prayed before the God of heaven,

5 And said, I beseech thee, O Lord God of heaven, the great and terrible God, that keepeth covenant and mercy for them that love him and observe his commandments:

6 Let thine ear now be attentive, and thine eyes open, that thou mayest hear the prayer of thy servant, which I pray before thee now, day and night, for the children of Israel thy servants, and confess the sins of the children of Israel, which we have sinned against thee: both I and my father's house have sinned.

He went on to pray for favor with the king. He wanted permission to go to Jerusalem, and timber to rebuild the walls and gates. The king granted him all that he requested.

This picture is one that the church needs to take to heart. When the walls of protection and safety in the body of Christ are torn and broken down, God is still looking for those to intercede and be used in the rebuilding.

Each generation needs its Nehemiahs that will respond to God's calling. God is not looking for ability, but for availability. He will provide the ability.

In each generation, God looks for a people who will rebuild and restore the walls of salvation. This ultimate salvation means deliverance from all temporal evil resulting from Satan being the god of this world system. Jesus purchased, redeemed, and freely made possible this ultimate salvation to all who believe on Him and receive the blessings of their covenant inheritance as children of Almighty God. Today, walls need to be repaired so that the church can walk in all of the benefits of salvation that Jesus has provided.

The gates of the city was the location where many things took place. Legal transactions, marketing, sharing news, and making business deals were typical activities at these gates. It was also the place where the king would sit and give audience for judgment on issues that were brought before him. Great importance, therefore, was put on making the gates secure.

The most vulnerable place along the walled city was its gates. Enemies would storm these gates to gain entry into the city and overtake it. Because of the power in the Name of Jesus, the gates of hell (the place of its authority), cannot prevail against the church that exercises its dominion, and has individual, personal revelation of Who Jesus, the Christ, is.

Nehemiah was called of God to restore the walls and rebuild the gates of Jerusalem. After receiving all that he needed from the king to accomplish the work, he met with open opposition from the enemy. In like manner, those in the body of Christ who receive a commission from the Lord, and provisions from the King of kings to do their part in restoring walls and gates, will meet with direct opposition from the enemy. The devil arrives on the scene and launches out a scheme to stop the work of the Lord Jesus Christ.

Almost immediately, Nehemiah had to contend with opposition from unbelievers.

NEHEMIAH 2:10

10 When Sanballat the Horonite, and Tobiah the servant, the Ammonite, heard of it, it grieved them exceedingly that there was come a man to seek the welfare of the children of Israel.

Nehemiah was not seeking his own welfare, but rather that of the children of Israel. He was comfortable in the palace, but he loved God and His people.

In reality, therefore, the opposition is against more than just an individual. It is opposition against an entire nation, a church, a family, or a ministry. The enemy is not coming for just one person, but for everyone connected with him.

The enemy's opposition is progressive and persistent. It is like the three areas of temptation, that is, lust, pride, and love of money. You will not be faced with just one of them, but all three. However, like Jesus, we have the weapons to overcome, and to stay in victory.

It is no shame to be faced with temptation of any kind. Instead, rejoice that you are counted worthy to be challenged. You do not have to yield, but you do need to recognize the opposition and stop it from overtaking you.

Spirit of Grief

The first opposition that Nehemiah encountered was the spirit of grief on Sanballat and Tobiah. In Hebrew, the word for "grieved" in this context is *rooa*, which literally means to do evil, to be wretched. It is the opposite of mercy.

In Hebrew one of the words for "mercy" is *rikham*, meaning to have compassion, and it is the same word for womb. That is where mercy originates. It comes out of the very "womb" of El Shaddai, the God who nourishes and provides for us. As grief encompasses every evil work, mercy encompasses every good work and blessing of Almighty God.

Grief is a curse. We cannot tolerate a spirit of grief even when someone dies. As an example, Ezekiel was not even permitted to attend his own wife's funeral, nor was he allowed to weep over his dead wife. This is not to say that sorrow does not attend death.

You cannot allow a spirit of grief to enter no matter who hurts you, no matter what is done, or isn't done. It is a root ruling spirit and out of it grows many undesirable things.

On one occasion of ministering at a pastors' meeting, a woman came forward for prayer, who I had known for years. Her child had never known his father because he is one of those listed as missing in action in Vietnam and was never found. He was pronounced dead, even though there was no evidence of it.

Before she was about to remarry, she called me for prayer and counsel. As I prayed for her, I saw her in a wedding dress with a bridal veil, but the color of her wedding garments were grey instead of white. I was very puzzled, but didn't say anything about it. Even though she married a fine man, and they tried hard, their marriage was just missing something. Stability and peace were not there. They did everything they knew to do, yet their victory was not complete.

As she stood before me in that prayer line she was sobbing. By the Spirit, I saw something that looked like a leek with little roots that had shoots coming out of it. I knew that if that thing was not cast out, it would come up and choke the very life out of her.

God showed me that the root of the problem was in great part due to grief. All the emotional entrapments of jealousy, confusion, worry, depression, and even physical infirmities, were all connected to her unresolved grief. She was set free that night, receiving total deliverance from the Lord.

The Holy Spirit covered this condition through Paul's message to the Thessalonians. In 1 Thessalonians 4:13, it says, "But I would not have you ignorant, brethren, concerning them which are asleep, that ye sorrow not, even as others which have no hope." Grief is sorrow without hope, but, we are "...of the hope and resurrection of the dead..."(Acts 23:6b).

When a loved one dies, it is natural to feel sorrow, to weep, and even perhaps have some regrets for a while. However, the spirit of grief cannot be allowed to linger because it precipitates other evil things. It creates heaviness, depression, discouragement and frustration, just to mention a few.

Counter-attack for Grief

The counter-attack for grief is the Word of God. In 1 Samuel 30, we see a mighty army built up under the direction of David. This army had been nothing more than a rag-tag bunch of disgruntled, distressed derelicts, but David made them into a powerful fighting machine. First Samuel 22:2 describes them as follows.

1 SAMUEL 22:2

2 **And every one that was in distress, and everyone that was in debt, and every one that was discontented, gathered themselves unto him; and he became a captain over them: and there were with him about four hundred men.**

They were fully confident in David's leadership as long as they were winning the battles. One day, however, they went off to battle and the enemy came into their camp. The camp was destroyed and their wives and children were taken captive. When David and his men returned, they found the wreckage and their families missing. The men were terribly grieved, that is, bitter of soul.

Suddenly, they turned on David, blaming him for their loss. The men needed a scapegoat, and they wanted to stone him to death. David became the target of their seeming defeat because their grief overtook all rationality.

What was David's response? He knew that his men were responding to grief. Nevertheless, he needed to respond in a way that would produce overcoming victory.

1 SAMUEL 30:6

6 And David was greatly distressed; for the people spake of stoning him, because the soul of all the people was grieved, every man for his sons and for his daughters: but David encouraged himself in the Lord his God.

✓ When grief comes against you, when bitterness tries to take root, when sorrow and disappointment makes you feel like everything is falling apart, don't yield to it. Go to the Lord as David did. No one can encourage you like Jesus, the Father, and the Holy Spirit. Encouraging yourself in the Lord is the answer to self-pity and frustration.

In James 5:13a, the question is asked, "Is any among you afflicted?..." The remedy is given immediately. It doesn't say to call the intercessors when you are grieved, cast down, discouraged, or sorely tried. It doesn't even say to call the pastor, or get the elders to anoint you with oil. Getting others to agree in prayer with you for specific things is fine, but when you are afflicted, James 5:13a says "...let him pray...."

Who is your strength? It cannot be flesh and blood, but it must be Almighty God. I can just hear you thinking, "Well, you know we all reach a point...", as you remember the last frustrating event that seemed insurmountable. If it was "nipped in the bud" when it first hit, it would not have grown to the point of desperation.

When grief, discouragement, or bitterness, tries to come, shut yourself away in the secret place of the Most High God like David did. If you are too busy to spend time daily with God, you will find that your time will be eaten up with the anxiety of this world. As Job said, "My days are swifter than a weaver's shuttle, and are spent without hope" (Job 7:6). No time for God means no hope.

God surely knows our schedules, but the time you devote to fellowship with God will result in the prevention of time wasted in aggravation. I would rather spend the time enjoying the Lord than fussing with the devil.

When you go to the Lord, what are you going to say? Will it be, "Lord, did you hear what they said about me? Did you see what they did to me and how they mistreated me?" The Lord is very merciful, compassionate, and knows what is troubling you before you even say anything. Follow the example of Acts 4:28,29 in prayer.

ACTS 4:28,29

28 For to do whatsoever thy hand and thy counsel determined before to be done.

29 And now, Lord, behold their threatenings: and grant unto thy servants, that with all boldness they may speak thy word,

Instead of complaining, spend the time expressing your love for Him, worshipping Him, and praying in the Spirit. It will break out of you like a bursting dam. In II Samuel 5:20a, it says, "...The Lord hath broken forth upon mine enemies before me, as the breach of waters...." The more you pray in the Holy Ghost, the more it is going to wash every bit of grief out of you.

Scorn, the Second Opposition

When Nehemiah arrived in Jerusalem, he first checked out the extent of the damage to the walls and the gates. Then he spoke to the rulers, priests, and workers.

NEHEMIAH 2:18,19

18 Then I told them of the hand of my God which was good upon me; as also the king's words that he had spoken unto me. And they said, Let us rise up and build. So they strengthened their hands for this good work.

19 But when Sanballat the Horonite, and Tobiah the servant, the Ammonite, and Geshem the Arabian, heard it, they laughed us to scorn, and despised us, and said, What is this thing that ye do? will ye rebel against the king?

Just when everyone was in agreement and it looked like there would be no more opposition, along comes the devil manipulating his servants to ridicule Nehemiah and try to stop the work of God.

No sooner does Nehemiah announce that he has favor with the king in regards to this project, than the three scorners challenge him on it. This is just like the devil's words to Eve, "...Yea, hath God said, Ye shall not eat of every tree of the garden?" (Genesis 3:1b) He wants to create confusion so that you begin to doubt even the things that you know are certain. The objective of laughing to scorn is to demoralize the person to the point where they shrivel up and have no more effectiveness. Have you experienced someone laughing at you for what you believed God wanted you to do? Have you heard them say, "You'll never amount to anything. You'll never be able to do that in this city. Your house will never come into divine order. Who do you think you're kidding?"

They might have even accused you of being prideful, saying, "Who do you think you are?" That was inspired by the devil to abort the work of the Lord before it even had begun. They don't trust you or God's ability to work through you. They are telling you that you are powerless, so you might as well give up.

At other times, you might have been targeted for laughter because of some calamity in your life. The devil rejoices at calamity, such as when a business deal goes sour. He mocks and derides in order to crush your enthusiasm and motivation to keep moving on in your life.

Laughter Is Medicine

Laughter is a powerful tool for destruction, but there is a laughter in the Holy Ghost that causes victory to be birthed. Proverbs 17:22 says, "A merry heart doeth good like a medicine...."

One time in Sweden, I ministered in fourteen power-packed services in eight days, after traveling between sixteen and nineteen hours to arrive there. After ministering, I had to travel the same amount of time to return home. It certainly was a rigorous schedule, one that would have left anyone exhausted. On the contrary, I felt like I had been on a two week vacation when I arrived home.

The entire time I was there, I didn't have time to take care of business matters, or to worry about anything. I hardly had time to dream because I was not sleeping long enough to dream. I didn't have time for frustration or hurt feelings on any level. I barely had time to eat the two meals a day, and do all that was necessary to prepare for the services.

My mind was fixed on the grace and glory of God, and the anointing on fellow ministers. We talked at length about what God was doing. We rejoiced and we praised God. There was dancing, shouting, and singing in the Spirit in the services. Miracles happened like never before as I ministered, and I saw the glory on God's people like I had never seen it.

The notable thing, though, was all of the laughter in the Holy Ghost. You can't fake that by a false pious spirit. There was a spirit of laughter that came in waves continuously.

One particular night, there were about two thousand people in attendance. The praise and worship was astounding, full of spirited singing, shouting, and dancing. After that, the choir marched up to the platform, and the director conducted the musicians and vocalists in Handel's "Hallelujah Chorus." The congregation entered into the chorus, and it was so glorious that one would have thought the rapture was taking place.

When that wave of worship subsided, another group went to the platform followed by another director. He was an African-American from South Carolina on assignment to this Swedish church. He began to direct these singers and the place became unglued. It was magnificent! You would have thought those Swedes were from Africa. It was about as opposite in style as you could get, from the "Hallelujah Chorus" to heavenly "soul" music, but it was the orchestration of God.

It was then time for me to minister the Word. Everything was ready, and I went up to the pulpit with my interpreter, who happened to be the pastor's associate minister.

Suddenly, I began to weep over a prophetic word that I was seeing for this young man. I prophesied over him, and he fell under the power of the Holy Spirit. I called the pastor forward, and he also fell under the power of God. Finally I did get another interpreter, but then I fell under the power of the Holy Spirit. When I was able to get up, I couldn't even stand. I knelt and prophesied in English, and the interpreter spoke it out in Swedish.

After that prophecy, God anointed me to walk down the aisles prophesying to several people. I was speaking out specific things for which they needed healing and deliverance. Each one was like reading an open book. People were weeping to my right and left, receiving what they needed from the Lord.

The reason that I was so refreshed instead of being exhausted, was because the laughter led of the Spirit was strong and frequent. Although there were some serious moments, the laughter was my medicine for fatigue.

On one of my visits, the Spirit of the Lord came upon me and I began to laugh. I put the microphone to the pastor's mouth, and he began to laugh. Then the whole congregation caught the laughter.

One morning soon after, the pastor was driving to church and was suddenly inspired to turn on his car radio, even though he otherwise never does so. A religious speaker was reporting over the radio that the people in this pastor's church were crazy, demonic people who laughed in church services. The speaker then went on to say that he would give evidence about his assertions on the next day's program.

This religious speaker had obtained a tape of the service where we were laughing, and they played it on the radio for one solid week, scorning and ridiculing it.

My pastor friend said, "When I heard that at first, I was upset, but as I heard myself laughing over the car radio, I was delivered from the oppression that the devil had been putting on me." You see, he suffers enormous persecution and threats on his life for the work that he is doing there.

The devil hates Spirit led laughter. He would much rather see you prune-faced and pitiful. Religious systems don't allow laughter because in religion, there is no liberty in the Spirit.

Holy Laughter

Another time when holy laughter came on me was in Israel, while touring the Dome of the Rock mosque in Jerusalem. Since that time, I have not entered it, nor do I permit any of the people on my Israel tour groups to enter the mosque. I found out since then, that removing your shoes and entering the mosque is giving homage to the god of that place. My homage belongs to Jesus Christ.

The custom of the Moslems required the tour members to remove their shoes and leave all of their purses and baggage outside of the mosque. I volunteered to stay outside in the midst of a mountain of assorted shoes, sandals, sneakers, handbags, and shopping bags, to guard their possessions while they had a look inside the mosque.

As the tour members came back, the whole scene suddenly became hilarious to me. I knew without a doubt that it was the Holy Spirit. I was bending back laughing, when some Moslem men converged on me and said, "Shhhh! No laugh — holy place, holy place — no laugh!"

The situation was quite serious because Moslems consider that place so sacred, they would protect it to their death, or mine. Instead of becoming sober, it struck me even funnier, and I just continued to laugh deep inside.

The tour group members hurriedly put on their shoes, grabbed their baggage, and pretended they didn't know me. It really was precarious and dangerous. Two faithful women helped me up and began to intercede over the situation. The laughter inside just didn't leave.

The group proceeded on to the place where they claim Abraham brought his son to be sacrificed. Now this was not irreverence, but when we arrived at that place, the spirit of laughter came strongly on me. They were helping me down the stairs, but I made it only to the fourth one when I just fell down on the stair and rolled back in laughter.

A thunderous noise came from the bottom of the steps. Like an army, some Moslem men came running towards me. I raised my head and came eyeball to eyeball with the leader of these men. With a jolt, he jerked backwards and said in awe, "What do you want with us?"

At first I didn't know what he was talking about, but then it struck me that this was the same question the demons asked Jesus. It stunned me and I was speechless. The man recovered from his clash with the Holy Spirit and said, "Shhh, no laugh, holy place," and then left along with the other men.

The tour guide came running back to me and said, "Do you know where you were? You were in front of the prison gate. They have put people in prison for less than what you were doing."

PSALM 2:1-4

1 Why do the heathen rage, and the people imagine a vain thing?

2 The kings of the earth set themselves, and the rulers take counsel together, against the Lord, and against his anointed, saying,

3 Let us break their bands asunder, and cast away their cords from us.

4 He that sitteth in the heavens shall laugh: the Lord shall have them in derision.

I believe I was laughing because the devil's time is short. I wasn't laughing at flesh and blood, but because the devil knows that his time is about up, and his hordes of demons that were coming after me knew it too.

When the devil laughs you to scorn, turn the tables and quit letting him get away with it. Job 5:22 says, "At destruction and famine thou shalt laugh: neither shalt thou be afraid of the beasts of the earth." Job found out some things about destruction and famine. When demonic calamities come at you, receive the spirit of laughter, and have the last laugh at the devil.

The devil particularly shows up when a person is determined in prayer. Nehemiah was a prayer warrior. He prayed for the rebuilding of the walls and the gates. When you as a prayer warrior pray about the walls of salvation and taking your city for God, it should not surprise you that the devil's cage gets rattled. When you are moving in the things of God, you most likely will encounter those who grieve, and those who attempt to laugh and scorn you to weakness and defeat. Rather than being discouraged, take the example of Nehemiah and press on to the call and work of God.

Nehemiah encountered four more oppositions as he continued his work in rebuilding the broken down walls and burned gates of Jerusalem. Those who seek to do the Lord's work deal with the same enemy tactics. They are as follows:

1. Wrath (Nehemiah 4:1-6)
2. Fighting and open opposition (Nehemiah 4:7-23)
3. A persistent enemy wanting a meeting with sabotage and treachery in their minds (Nehemiah 6:1-9)
4. False friends (Nehemiah 6:10-14)

As you seek the Holy Spirit, He will give you wisdom, knowledge, and understanding concerning such warfare against your victory in Jesus.

The Ruling Spirit Causes Opposition

While ministering one time in Nashville, Tennessee, a man came forward and expressed that he was very troubled. He said that during the praise and worship, he had seen a huge black snake wrapped around the piano. He didn't understand what he was seeing.

Later in conversation with the pastor of that church, I told him what the man said, and then explained about the python spirit. I told him how it is like a python snake that is camouflaged in trees, and then falls on its victim suddenly, squeezing the life out of them with strong constricting muscles.

Then I related how it works in churches. The church leaders begin working in a locale, and just when the congregation grows in number to a respectable size of about one hundred, the people get squeezed out by all sorts of demon inspired work.

As I spoke, the pastor said, "Bobbie Jean, you are exactly right. The praise and worship in this church used to be great, and then it would subside. Then it would build up, and again would subside. It just keeps going in cycles of great and mediocre." It was the python spirit at work opposing God's work.

On a national level, the spirit of python has been identified. As you ride the streets of Washington, D.C., you will notice every kind of cult activity, idol worship, and religion imaginable, to say nothing of the pornography and other unmentionable horrors.

A couple who are pastoring a church in Washington, D.C., were made aware of some horrendous satanic activity in one of the buildings in the area. Some of their church members walked around it praying that if it could not be purified, then it would have to be demolished. Satanic activity does not go on there any longer, because the building has been razed. There is power in unified prayer against the works of the devil.

In March of 1980, I spent considerable time in Israel. I met missionaries there that were truly called to Israel. They suffered terribly from "battle fatigue," yet they refused to leave for recuperation. They became irrational and unreasonable. They were not much good to their families or anyone else, yet they would not budge out of Israel.

Their effectiveness was squeezed out. The spirit of python seeks to squeeze the life out of anyone or anything in whatever fashion it can. One of his ways is to wear out God's ministers in continuous work without taking time for rest and refreshing for the spirit, soul, and body.

There is a happy ending to this story. As some of these missionaries were strengthened by the Word of God, and receiving the anointing, the eyes of their understanding were opened. After I left Israel, they sought the Lord concerning the timing of their ministry in Israel. He directed them to return to their homeland, America, and they obeyed.

Paul and Silas met up with the ruling spirit of python in Philippi, Macedonia in Acts 16:16-26. It was Paul's first missionary trip to Europe. It is interesting to note that the masters of the girl who was delivered from the spirit of divination were upset because of their loss of profit. It is interesting to note that the Macedonian church ended up being great givers. They understood the ministry of giving and operated in the grace of giving. (Compare 2 Corinthians 8 and 9.)

Python is largely connected with divination, that is, trying to discover future events by superstitious means. However, it motivates its operatives with the love of money, the root of all evil. With believers, it wants to squeeze the money out from your hands, so that it can squeeze out the ministry. When people cut off their financial giving, it serves as a blow to the work of the ministry.

The focus of divination is on prediction of future events, basically so that one could control circumstances to one's advantage. There is more attention on the future, and less on the now. It is a diversionary tactic that gets people looking to tomorrow, and never accomplishing what God wants for today. In every way it is opposition to God's work.

Proverbs 14:12 says, "There is a way which seemeth right unto a man, but the end thereof are the ways of death." This statement defines deception. Everything appears true and correct, yet beneath it all there is nothing but destruction.

Python Attacks Your Mantle

When people do not respect divine order of government and authority, it is a working of the python spirit.

The opposite of government or authority is anarchy. That's when each person is a law unto himself. It causes chaos, isolation, and loss of protection.

Lawlessness is when an individual has no regard for the ramifications of his actions toward other people. Every decision and action is centered around the question of "What is in this for me?"

MATTHEW 7:21-23

21 Not every one that saith unto me, Lord, Lord, shall enter into the kingdom of heaven; but he that doeth the will of my Father which is in heaven.

22 Many will say to me in that day, Lord, Lord, have we not prophesied in thy name? and in thy name have cast out devils? and in thy name done many wonderful works?

23 And then will I profess unto them, I never knew you: depart from me, ye that work iniquity.

Those who are workers of iniquity are lawless. Jesus was addressing underlying motives and attitudes. In essence, He was saying, "You prophesy and cast out devils to make a name or profit for yourselves. You are only interested in what benefits you and you are not interested in doing the will of God for His glory."

People who recognize the divine order of God know that church leaders are not there to be lords and masters over the people. The mantle is what protects the one called to be in the position of leadership. When python is permitted to enter by disrespect for authority, it attempts to squeeze you out of that position and protection.

The devil is after the mantles on those anointed to serve. Ezekiel 28, describes Lucifer's magnificent covering before his fall.

EZEKIEL 28:13-15 (Jerusalem Bible)

13 you were in Eden, in the garden of God. A thousand gems formed your mantle. Sard, topaz, diamond, chrysolite, onyx, jasper, sapphire, carbuncle, emerald, the gold of which your flutes and tambourines are made, all were prepared on the day of your creation.

14 I had provided you with a guardian cherub; you were on the holy mountain of God; you walked amid red-hot coals.

15 Your behavior was exemplary from the day of your creation until the day when evil was first found in you.

He was anointed in leading the praise and worship of God. In him was fullness of music. This is why he has corrupted music. He inspires the seductive, beguiling perversions of music that cause people to behave like barbarians.

His mantle was magnificent and beautiful beyond description. He was the anointed cherub, and his mantle was so glorious that vanity gripped his loyalty to God. He wanted all of the glory for himself. His attack on government and authority is based in his passion for glory.

Because of the accomplished work of Jesus, he has no song or joy in him, and he is stripped bare. He is tone deaf and naked. He wants your covering, your mantle, your anointing.

Ultimately, if we let go of our mantle, we let go of our life. Our mantle is the good, acceptable, perfect will and call of God for our life. That is why David could not wear Saul's armor. It didn't fit him, and he needed to move within the mantle that God had for him. It was his life and his protection. Each of us has a call, an anointing, a mantle that fits us just perfectly and gives us total satisfaction in Christ. Nothing else will fit or satisfy us until we walk in His perfect will.

Satan wants what he lost. He lost the government of praise and worship, the song of the Lord, his anointing, and his mantle. He wants to steal these from God's anointed vessels, but you don't have to let him. You have authority in the Name of Jesus to stop any plots or schemes that he may try.

Chapter 5
Beguiling Spirits

When God brought the nation of Israel out of Egyptian bondage, it was not just because they had a need. God led them out to serve and obey Him.

When Jeremiah received the call of God, the Lord said to him, "See, I have this day set thee over the nations and over the kingdoms, to root out, and to pull down, and to destroy, and to throw down, to build, and to plant" (Jeremiah 1:10). He had a specific purpose, to upset the kingdom of darkness, and put things right according to God's kingdom.

In like manner, believers have been redeemed out of Satan's bondage to unconditionally serve and obey Almighty God. First John 3:8 says of Jesus, "...For this purpose the Son of God was manifested, that he might destroy the works of the devil." As believers, having power and authority in Jesus, we have also been called to destroy the works of the devil.

National Symptoms of Python's Work

In our nation, we have seen wonderful works of God begin, grow beautifully, and then suddenly experience the blow of a church split. Marriages move along blissfully, and then one day you hear that the couple is in divorce court. Businesses are prospering and expanding, and then seemingly out of nowhere you find them in bankruptcy.

The lives of children were once valued and cherished as part of our national morality. Yet babies are being destroyed by the thousands daily in abortion clinics. Many times abortion is used as a remedy for the product of promiscuity. Women have been deceived into believing that they have ultimate determination over the life of another human being. Public outcry over capital punishment has not extended to the death sentence over innocent children. It's the same spirit that manifested in the days of the worship of Baal and Ashteroth, where babies were sacrificed on altars of fire.

Satanic worship and all manner of witchcraft among our youth is rising at an alarming rate. Teens are experimenting with demonic rituals and powers of darkness in alarming proportions. They are searching for meaning in their lives and power for living. They desperately need to know God and the power of the Holy Spirit.

Subtle Deception

Cults are arising that seem to defy description. They no longer look like tunic clad hippies with love beads and flower painted faces. Many have found the advantages of looking respectable, enticing new prey with subtle treachery. For example, New Age, with its various disguises and celebrity proponents, is nothing more than a modern version of ancient religions of divination controlled by the python spirit. There is nothing really new about it.

God is alerting those in this nation who have an ear to hear the Spirit of the Lord. Ephesians 5:11 tells us, "And have no fellowship with the unfruitful works of darkness, but rather reprove them." To reprove them means to expose the works of the devil. We don't have to be intimidated. By the power of the Holy Spirit, we bring the light of the gospel that dispels and swallows up the darkness.

2 CORINTHIANS 11:3,4

3 But I fear, lest by any means, as the serpent beguiled Eve through his subtilty, so your minds should be corrupted from the simplicity that is in Christ.

4 For if he that cometh preacheth another Jesus, whom we have not preached, or if ye receive another spirit, which ye have not received, or another gospel, which ye have not accepted, ye might well bear with him.

The third verse is so clear about where the battle-ground is located. The mind is that which can be corrupted. Subtle suggestions that deviate from the knowledge of God and His Word can creep in quietly. Much like a small deviation from the correct course in piloting an airplane at the beginning of the flight, can cause it to land far from the intended destination unless a correction is made.

I have read one New Age newspaper containing information about Jesus Christ, but let me caution you that "a" truth is not always "the" truth. In quoting from John 14:6, this newspaper advertised Jesus as "the way, the truth, and the light," to gain acceptability and allure unsuspecting readers into thinking it is something other than what it really is.

Cults do not take the whole counsel of God's Word, but rather selectively take scriptural statements out of context, to prove that which is far from "the" truth. Yes, Jesus is the light of the world that came to destroy the works of darkness, but John 14:6 actually says, "Jesus saith unto him, I am the way, the truth, and the life: no man cometh unto the Father, but by me."

Because this cult makes much of false light and false peace, they misquoted the Scriptures as bait and entrapment. This is only one example of seducing deception in operation.

In our generation, probably as never before, it may be said of us that unless we know God's Word thoroughly, we can be an open target for deception. Unless it agrees with God's Word in its entirety, it is a lie from the devil.

Beguiling to Seduce Believers From Devotion to Jesus

The *Amplified Bible* presents further illumination. It says, in 2 Corinthians 11:3, "But [now] I am fearful, lest that even as the serpent beguiled Eve by his cunning, so your minds may be corrupted and seduced from wholehearted and sincere and pure devotion to Christ." Notice the word "cunning" with reference to the devil. The enemy is subtle and clever to distort your understanding, and most especially, to attack your devotion to Jesus.

One of the most frequently asked questions that comes up among church leaders has to do with the apparent lack of commitment of individuals. People will attend church on Sunday morning looking so pious, yet they fail to live like a Christian for the rest of the week. Others receive the Lord and the baptism of the Holy Spirit, are excited and faithful for a while, and then they vanish.

The fifth chapter of Ephesians compares the relationship of Christ to the church with the relationship of a married couple. When two people love each other enough to marry, they enter into the marriage with the intent to stay together.

In like manner, we are the body of Christ and have an eternal relationship. What happens to the commitment, faithfulness, and the enthusiasm in the marriage or church relationship? When the participants hold fast and nurture it, there is steadfast growth in the relationship.

On the local church level, I have seen that God is establishing the local church as never before in this generation. Nevertheless, we see that the enthusiasm wanes, the faithfulness becomes erratic, and the commitment erodes.

It has been called a spirit of stupor, spirit of laziness, or lack of commitment. Preachers have been told, "You just need to preach and teach another seminar on commitment." I submit to you that it is a beguiling spirit that is working against the marriage of Jesus to the church.

Whether in a marriage or connecting into a local church body, the individual starts out intent in their devotion to that mate, or devotion to the Lord Jesus Christ in serving Him in that congregation. The priority is sincere, wholehearted devotion. What is really happening when that individual starts to lose commitment, faithfulness, enthusiasm, and wholehearted devotion? It is the beguiler at work and the individual has yielded to his influence.

God does not tell us that something is wrong and leave it to us to find a solution. In His Word, He tells us how to overcome and maintain the victory.

When the beguiler is at work, he draws you away from the natural affection of the one you love. He draws people away from their fellowship in the church. We cannot permit the devil to take any ground in drawing us away from the simplicity of the gospel of Jesus Christ.

God desires unity of the faith, and of the knowledge of the Son of God. Jesus prayed for that unity in John 17:21, "That they all may be one; as thou, Father, art in me, and I in thee, that they also may be one in us: that the world may believe that thou hast sent me." How are we going to win the world? When we walk in unity in Christ, the work of the evangelist gets done.

Life Is in the Blood

Every cult or religion that rises up from the beginning to the end of time will be destroyed for one reason. It does not produce life. Something that is not alive cannot produce life in others, nor does it have eternal life. It does not have the foundation of life, Jesus Christ.

The Old Testament is very explicit about the blood of animals in sacrifice, but these offerings were inadequate and needed to be repeated again and again, because there could not be a perfect animal. There could not even be a perfect human sacrifice because all had sinned. Ancient religious cults had human sacrifice, but it was not sufficient to satisfy the demands of a perfect redemption for mankind. It took the pure and sinless blood of the Lord Jesus Christ, willingly given once for all mankind forever. There is life in His blood and it produces life in us.

EZEKIEL 16:6

6 And when I passed by thee, and saw thee polluted in thine own blood, I said unto thee when thou wast in thy blood, Live; yea, I said unto thee when thou wast in thy blood, Live.

The only way your polluted blood will become cleansed is by the pure blood of the Lord Jesus Christ.

Buddha is dead; Mohammed is dead; Zeus and Apollo are not only dead, they never lived. New Agers, Rainbow People, and whatever else may come on the scene, will also die, but the blood of Jesus has life eternal. We don't need a "channel." We have the Way, the Truth, and the Life, and His Name is Jesus.

Many voices are shouting "Peace," but there is only one place to obtain peace. Everything that was necessary to give us peace was laid on the back of Jesus as was declared in Isaiah 53:5.

ISAIAH 53:5

5 But he was wounded for our transgressions, he was bruised for our iniquities: the chastisement of our peace was upon him; and with his stripes we are healed.

The voices that cry out that peace is here, or peace is there, challenge you to try weird techniques for experiencing the supernatural. Beware of this pseudo-peace. God is a Mighty Warrior. There is no peace in the heavenlies. There is a battle raging and you have an active enemy that wants to pound you to dust. There is only one real peace that is lasting and never changing, and that is in the presence of the Prince of Peace, Jesus Christ.

Promise of Life

In Genesis 3:15, God prophesies ultimate doom to the enemy who beguiled Eve. He said, "And I will put enmity between thee and the woman, and between thy seed and her seed; it shall bruise thy head, and thou shalt bruise his heel."

All cults and false religious systems promise life, but there is only One Who gives life, and that is Jesus Christ. As John 1:4 tells us, "In him was life; and the life was the light of men." Anything else is deception.

Understanding Grace

Most of us think of grace as unmerited favor. To a very limited definition, that is true. However, grace is that and so much more. Grace is the ability, strength, help, sufficiency, efficiency, and power of God. Grace for you and me is none other than the Holy Spirit, Himself, in manifestation.

Being an overcomer and staying victorious over beguiling spirits is walking in the grace to obey God's Word. Paul had learned this powerful lesson. In the seventh chapter of Romans, he points out man's weakness and inability to overcome sin, and describes the devil as the master of sin. Paul said that his flesh did not want to obey what his spirit wanted him to do, but then adds the key verse, "I thank God through Jesus Christ our Lord..." (Romans 7:25a).

The grace of God flows through our Lord Jesus Christ. He, Himself, points the way to receiving grace. "Watch and pray, that you enter not into temptation: the spirit indeed is willing, but the flesh is weak" (Matthew 26:41). The writer of Hebrews 4:16 confirms this by inviting us to "...come boldly unto the throne of grace, that we may obtain mercy, and find grace to help in time of need."

Paul, like us, often found himself weak and in need of resources beyond what he could supply for himself. He concluded, "...of myself I will not glory, but in mine infirmities" (2 Corinthians 12:5). He could say this because God had spoken to him.

2 CORINTHIANS 12:9,10

9 And he said unto me, My grace is sufficient for thee: for my strength is made perfect in weakness. Most gladly therefore will I rather glory in my infirmities, that the power of Christ may rest upon me.

10 Therefore I take pleasure in infirmities, in reproaches, in necessities, in persecutions, in distresses for Christ's sake: for when I am weak, then am I strong.

Those who you know are walking in victory, are doing so by the grace of God. Therefore, we must not confuse the earthen vessel with the treasure that is in it.

Many people have been receiving the vessel in ministry instead of the anointing that is in the vessel, preferring flesh over the Holy Spirit.

Never glory in flesh. Too many men and women have been exalted instead of the anointing of Almighty God. It has caused some to fall hard. God will not share His glory with flesh, "That, according as it is written, He that glorieth, let him glory in the Lord" (1 Corinthians 1:31). It takes obedience to the Word of God by His grace to walk in liberty.

Whatever we do in living victoriously over beguiling spirits or any other spirits for that matter, we will do by grace. You will never be able to tackle the powers of darkness in your own strength, knowledge, or ability. It takes grace operating in your life. The good news is that the grace of the Holy Spirit is freely accessible to all who believe.

Destroying from Within

Some of you may be saying to yourself, "I thought this was going to be about overcoming principalities, powers, spiritual wickedness in the heavenly places, the rulers of darkness, strongholds, and even Satan, himself." Well, you are absolutely correct.

One of the things we can learn from studying the civilizations mentioned in the Bible, is that unless we learn the lessons of history, we may find ourselves reliving them. The Roman civilization, powerful and expansive as it was, did not fall apart entirely because of external circumstances. It was destroyed from within. The decay worked from the inside to the outside. Even though this is an example from the natural world, a pagan one at that, there is a principle worth noting and heeding.

As Christians, we need to get ourselves straightened out personally, and in the local church first. How can you destroy that which is on the outside, when there is no power working on the inside? If you are going to be like a chain saw against the enemy, you need fuel and power to do it.

The Battleground

First of all, we can recognize the inner working and deteriorating effects of beguiling spirits in attitudes and thought life. If beguiling spirits are working against you, there will be a sense that the simplicity of Jesus is eroding. The pure, wholehearted, sincere devotion to Him begins to wane. The excitement, enthusiasm, and expectancy for the presence of God the Father, the Son, and the Holy Spirit begins to dwindle, as well as the zeal for the work of the local church body. The same applies to other areas of your life including home and family relationships.

The battleground, therefore, is an interior one. It is in your mind, the soul realm. Once identified, how are you going to overcome it? You are not going to conquer the external until the internal is under control.

2 CORINTHIANS 10:4-6 (Amplified Bible)

4 For the weapons of our warfare are not physical [weapons of flesh and blood], but they are mighty before God for the overthrow and destruction of strongholds,

5 [Inasmuch as we] refute arguments and theories and reasonings and every proud and lofty thing that sets itself up against the [true] knowledge of God; and we lead every thought and purpose away captive into the obedience of Christ, (the Messiah, the Anointed One),

6 Being in readiness to punish every [insubordinate for his] disobedience, when your own submission and obedience [as a church] are fully secured and complete.

Every outward work starts with an inward work in the mind. It was Eve's mind that was beguiled. God had already said that they would die if they ate of the tree of the knowledge of good and evil. Then Satan came offering promises of life and telling Eve that she would not die. It was all a play on her mind. She entertained the suggestion in her mind, her mouth spoke it out, and her actions carried it out in quick succession.

Second Corinthians 10:5 tells us that we can come to the place of taking every thought and submitting it to the obedience of Jesus. It says, "Casting down imaginations, and every high thing that exalteth itself against the knowledge of God, and bringing into captivity every thought to the obedience of Christ;" thereby rendering it helpless. How do you do this?

When a thought comes to you that you know is not pleasing to Jesus, say to the enemy, "Devil, it is written in 2 Corinthians 10:5, that I can cast down this thought. It does not belong to me because it exalts itself against the knowledge of God. Jesus died that I might be free from that thought. That thought was laid on Jesus when He became sin for me." Just picture that thought being laid on Jesus. It is now no longer yours and cannot hurt you. Do this until you have the victory.

Team that up with Romans 6:11, which says, "Likewise reckon ye also yourselves to be dead indeed unto sin, but alive unto God through Jesus Christ our Lord." Do you know what "reckon" means? It means to judge or regard as being already done. Whether you see it or not, you reckon the sun will come up tomorrow morning. In the same way, consider any wrong thought to be dead and laid on Jesus when He became sin for us. Reckon it to be dead. This will bring victory to you.

Meaning of Beguile

What does beguile mean? It means to deceive. In James 1:22 it says, "But be ye doers of the word, and not hearers only, deceiving your own selves." We have the ability to deceive ourselves when our faith is not in action. Unconditional obedience to the Word of God, not just hearing, but doing, keeps deception at bay. If you are not a "doer" of what you hear or read in God's Word, you are a candidate for deception, error, and a beguiling spirit. One way to destroy the operation of beguiling spirits is to be a "doer" of the Word.

Beguile also means to catch by bait. My husband, Milton, is a bass fisherman. However, in his many times of fishing, he has never had a bass jump into his boat. He puts bait on a hook. When the hook and bait go into the water, the bait is disguised as food for the unsuspecting bass fish. The fish bites what it thinks is a real morsel of food. It isn't the bait that catches the fish, it's the hook.

When Satan operates against someone, he uses bait. He lures the person with something so that he can destroy the person. He doesn't show you his hook. He is far more clever than that. He covers and disguises it with bait.

The bait is different for each person. What is alluring to one person, would never interest another. He knows what it would take to tempt the person away from the simple gospel of the Lord Jesus Christ to another "Messiah." If it doesn't look, think, walk, talk, or act like Jesus Christ, it's bait. The end result is death, not life.

Beguile means to entice. How does adultery, fornication, homosexuality, or lesbianism get a grip? It works the same way that fear or bait does. Somebody gets your attention and entices you. You begin to devote much thought life to that person and allow desire for that person to increase. It is bait drawing you like a magnet. Even fear will draw itself to you, but so will faith if you let it.

Be aware of the enemy's plan for your soul. At the onset of a thought that is ungodly, say, "I'm taking my eyes off of that. I'm looking unto Jesus, the Author and Finisher of my faith." Your steps will then go in the right direction. Is He enough? He is El Shaddai. He is more than enough. He is the All-Sufficient One who satisfies all that you need. He is Jesus, the Christ, the Anointed One, the One who destroys every yoke of bondage.

Division in the Body

Beguiling spirits can work to cause divisions in the body of Christ at all levels. Division that is contrary to sound doctrine and that does not exalt Jesus, is a sure sign of beguiling spirits at work. Romans 16:17,18 cau-. tions us,

ROMANS 16:17,18

17 Now I beseech you, brethren, mark them which cause divisions and offences contrary to the doctrine which ye have learned; and avoid them.

18 For they that are such serve not our Lord Jesus Christ, but their own belly; and by good words and fair speeches deceive the hearts of the simple.

The good words and fair speeches are the bait that beguiles people away from the Lord Jesus Christ. Eloquence of speech, good sounding programs, or even a string of degrees and titles, are not indicators of truth or anointing. Anointed servants of God may coincidentally have degrees or good programs, but the anointing comes from God, not man. In all cases, the Lord Jesus Christ must be exalted.

Deceitful Teachers

The beguiling spirit uses people to set a trap for the body of Christ. Back in the 1940's, we were told by the leading psychologists of the day that it was harmful to correct, discipline, or spank your baby. The prevailing thought was to allow the little darling to do whatever he or she wanted to do, since spanking would warp his or her personality. God's Word tells us to discipline our children lovingly, not to abuse them. We are to use the Word and the rod with wisdom because it drives out rebellion.

As a result of false psychological theory during the 1940's, the permissiveness of the parents of "baby boomers" turned out to be the greatest child abuse. We saw the social revolution of the 1960's drive those same children to mindless drug experimentation and gross sexual promiscuity from which we have not yet recovered.

The church was not left unscathed. The rebellion against all authority that we witnessed on college campuses was also found in the church. It evolved into some preachers keeping a very low profile on preaching and in order to keep the church full, they entertained the people. God is finished with entertainment. Religion will entertain you, but remember that there is no anointing to destroy the yoke of bondage in entertainment.

Religion and theory came into the church and said, "Don't rebuke me; don't chasten me; don't reprove me; just let me do what I want to do because there is therefore no condemnation." However, they didn't finish Romans 8:1, which says, "There is therefore now no condemnation to them which are in Christ Jesus, who walk not after the flesh, but after the Spirit." The Holy Spirit will certainly not lead us into sin or disobedience. He will lead us to be like Jesus.

As a result of wanting to pacify itching ears, the "I don't like it, and I'll go somewhere else" attitude, much of the church lost its rebuke, reproof, correction, and finally its leadership.

Someone who really loves you will say, "Hey, you're about to take the bait. The hook is disguised to bring you out of the kingdom of light into the kingdom of darkness." Love tells you when something is wrong because it seeks to preserve your life. God is love, and He loves us so much that He wants to keep us from dying.

False teachers, under the influence of beguiling spirits, want to lure you away from the truth of Christ. Titus 1:10,11 says,

TITUS 1:10,11

10 For there are many unruly and vain talkers and deceivers, specially they of the circumcision:

11 Whose mouths must be stopped, who subvert whole houses, teaching things which they ought not, for filthy lucre's sake.

Deception results in subversive destruction in the body of Christ. It is the power of darkness deceiving the minds of men and women to stop the kingdom of God from accomplishing what it has been called to do.

The beguiling spirits cause people to wander, go astray, and to cheat. Ultimately it cheats the person out of the things that Almighty God has for them by all manner of unscrupulous words and deeds.

Beguiling Spirits Entertain

Beguiling means to charm, to divert, to cause to vanish. The fact is, the devil would really like you to disappear off the face of the earth, but that won't happen to you with the power of God working on your behalf. Beguiling spirits entertain you with the objective of ensnaring and misleading you. Second Timothy 4:3,4 in the *Amplified Bible* says,

2 TIMOTHY 4:3,4 (Amplified Bible)

3 For the time is coming when [people] will not [tolerate] sound and wholesome instruction, but having ears itching [for something pleasing and gratifying], they will gather to themselves one teacher after another to a considerable number, chosen to satisfy their own liking and to foster the errors they hold,

4 And will turn aside from hearing the truth and wander off into myths and man-made fictions.

That is how heresies and cults gain a following from among believers as well as unbelievers.

Jeremiah 10:2 clearly addresses the same issue. It says, "Thus saith the Lord, Learn not the way of the heathen, and be not dismayed at the signs of heaven; for the heathen are dismayed at them." You don't need to learn about New Age thinking or any other religion. How much time do you have to study and read? Instead of spending time reading about false doctrine and pagan religions, spend that time studying and reading that which will produce life for you, God's Word.

We don't have to be dismayed at the movement of stars and planets. The heathens are dismayed and feel the need to appease their angry god by sacrificing children, or putting hooks into their flesh, or crawling on their knees on pavement until their hands and knees are bloody. If we served some hideous monster, we would be dismayed as well.

We are not afraid of idols who are served and worshipped as gods. "...Be not afraid of them; for they cannot do evil, neither also is it in them to do good" (Jeremiah 10:5b). We do not have to fear the devil either.

God's Goodness is His Manifested Glory

Glory to God, we are not dismayed. God's Word tells us that He is a covenant-keeping God, Who is always there to sustain and protect His own. God is a good and merciful God. The kingdom of His dear Son, Jesus Christ, is the kingdom of light and love, and in Him there is the power to bring us out of darkness into the light. We then have access freely into His very presence, and to experience His glory.

EXODUS 33:19

19 And he said, I will make all my goodness pass before thee, and I will proclaim the name of the Lord before thee; and will be gracious to whom I will be gracious, and will shew mercy on whom I will shew mercy.

How do you know when the glory is manifested? It is when His goodness is manifested. God will fight your battles when you are firm and confident in Him without fear. In Exodus 14:13,14, Moses declared the salvation of their God to the people of Israel as they stood between the sea and the approaching Egyptian army.

EXODUS 14:13,14

13 And Moses said unto the people, Fear ye not, stand still, and see the salvation of the Lord, which he will shew to you to day: for the Egyptians whom ye have seen to day, ye shall see them again no more for ever.

14 The Lord shall fight for you, and ye shall hold your peace.

We are to remain in faith's rest, knowing that our God will fight for us. Do everything you know to do, that is, study and meditate on God's Word, pray, destroy the works of the flesh, and then just enter into His rest.

The Lord told Moses to stop crying out to Him, but to tell the children of Israel to go forward. This is the challenge of the Holy Spirit. The ruling spirit over this nation has been Python, and with it the Jezebel, beguiling, and seducing spirits, and the church has been crying out, complaining, and pleading with God. God is saying, "Just go forward, Christian soldier."

When Moses was called by God to be the one who would lead his people out of the land of Egypt, he complained to God that he could not speak. God gave him a mouthpiece, his brother, Aaron. He then discovered that he could do nothing without the grace of God and that he needed to have a sign. He needed something to set him apart from the Satanists operating in Pharaoh's court. God took a simple staff and used it to perform signs and wonders.

When you decide that you can do nothing without the grace of God in doing what He has called you to do, He gives you the "rod" of power and anointing. It is a sign that the gates of hell recognize and fear.

When you operate in your gift and anointing, under your mantle, the gates of hell move and you prevail against them. God has given you something very specific, and when you operate in that gift, it stops the operation of hell in that situation. It may be a word for your brother, wisely spoken, at just the right time. Like Aaron's budding rod, it represents life and all that is in it, peace, true prosperity, and victory.

For another it may be a word that will calm troubled waters, or that will open the "Red Sea" of their life and they'll walk over on dry land. The same sea of difficulty or circumstance they have crossed to freedom, will now destroy their enemy, even as the Red Sea destroyed the armies of Pharaoh as they pursued the children of Israel.

You may have a gift of sending people nice cards. Only God knows what a card with one little meaningful sentence sent at the right time has done to liberate that person from the very onslaught of Satan. It might be just letting your light shine. Your rod might be intercessory prayer, or a gift of the Holy Spirit, or sharing the Word of God. Whatever it is, stretch it forth.

How are we going to overcome Python? We will do it by each of the unique, particular, valuable, and special individuals in the body of Christ, taking in their hands what God has given them and functioning as they should. As Moses was commanded, stretch forth thine hand. It is the anointing and the Holy Spirit.

EXODUS 14:26 (Amplified Bible)

26 Then the Lord said to Moses, Stretch out your hand over the sea, that the waters may come again upon the Egyptians, upon their chariots and horsemen.

Here is where we have sometimes missed it. Once the people were on the other side, Moses had to stretch forth his hand again to defeat the enemy. We need to finish the work of the warfare. We need to be alert and not give up.

By comparing Exodus 14:29 and Isaiah 43:2, we see the complete protection of God in the most trying situation.

EXODUS 14:29 (Amplified Bible)

29 But the Israelites walked on dry ground in the midst of the sea, the waters being a wall to them on their right hand and on their left.

ISAIAH 43:2 (Amplified Bible)

2 When you pass through the waters I will be with you, and through the rivers they shall not overwhelm you; when you walk through the fire you shall not be burned or scorched, nor shall the flame kindle upon you.

Who was responsible for the great victory of the Israelites on that momentous day? It was the Lord's doing. We are simply asked to hold out the rod, and watch the salvation of the Lord. You know that you could not save yourself. However, in obedience just be and do whatever God directs, and let Him do it.

There was great rejoicing among Moses and the Israelites on that day of victory. Moses sang out, "Who is like unto thee, O Lord, among the gods?..." (Exodus 15:11). This is our noblest and highest praise, recognizing the majesty and incomparable greatness of our God. As Moses prayed a blessing on the nation of Israel just before his death, he said,

DEUTERONOMY 33:26-29

26 There is none like unto the God of Jeshurun, who rideth upon the heaven in thy help, and in his excellency on the sky.

27 The eternal God is thy refuge, and underneath are the everlasting arms: and he shall thrust out the enemy from before thee; and shall say, Destroy them.

28 Israel then shall dwell in safety alone: the fountain of Jacob shall be upon a land of corn and wine; also his heavens shall drop down dew.

29 Happy art thou, O Israel: who is like unto thee, O people saved by the Lord, the shield of thy help, and who is the sword of thy excellency! and thine enemies shall be found liars unto thee; and thou shalt tread upon their high places.

If you want to have victory over any demonic spirit, you must ever recognize, and be keenly aware of the Name of the Lord. It is that Name alone that will bring you the victory, help you possess it and keep it.

PSALM 20 (Amplified Bible)

1 The Lord answer you in the day of trouble! The name of the God of Jacob set you up on high [and defend you];

2 Send you help from the sanctuary, and support, refresh and strengthen you from Zion;

3 Remember all your offerings, and accept your burnt sacrifice; Selah [pause, and think of that]!

4 Grant you according to your heart's desire, and fulfill all your plans.

5 We will (shout in) triumph at your salvation and victory, and in the name of our God we will set up our banners; the Lord fulfill all your petitions.

6 Now know I that the Lord saves His anointed; He will answer him from His holy Heaven with the saving strength of His right hand.

7 Some trust in and boast of chariots, and some of horses; but we will trust in and boast of the name of the Lord our God.

8 They are bowed down and fallen; but we are risen, and stand upright.

9 O Lord, give victory; let the King answer us when we call.

The Lord, Jehovah, is in covenant relation with His people, and His Names reveal that provision of His covenant which applies to His promise. In Psalm 20:1, God's defending Name is used. When we call on His Name, He defends us. It's just that simple. People want to complicate it, but instead of trying to prove how great we are, we just need to trust in the power of God's Name.

In Psalm 20:5, His Name is our banner, the *displayed* Name. We don't have to display the works of Satan. Talk about God and His goodness. He is the One Who fulfills our petitions.

In verse seven, we find the *delivering* Name of God. Some people boast in the strength of their might, their armies, their goods. We must not even boast in the strength of our intercessors, or ministers. If we boast at all, it should be in the Name of the Lord our God.

We may have been looking for some formulas, things to say or repeat. If you want your prayers to be heard; if you want to see the delivering hand of Almighty God, turn away from all that is evil and in obedience to Him, stretch forth the rod believing in His delivering power, and go forward. It's time to follow Jesus one step and one day at a time. Thank God for it in Jesus' Name.

Chapter 6
Seducing Spirits

Over the years of ministry, I have traveled to many parts of our country as well as abroad. I have noticed that when Christians become disproportionately fascinated and absorbed with demons and deliverance, they lose a positive perspective of the gospel.

They begin to view people, places, and things with negative, judgmental attitudes. They even interpret scripture with a sense of doom and foreboding. It can be summed up as being influenced by demonic forces that keeps them so preoccupied with darkness, that they forget that Jesus is the Light.

Discerning of spirits is a gift of the Holy Spirit, which allows you to see into the spiritual world. It allows you to perceive evil spirits, as well as angelic beings and God's supernatural workings. Prophets and seers frequently have this gift operating as they minister, however, it is not exclusively for them. The Holy Spirit is the one who directs the operation of His gifts.

The revelation and illumination received by the Spirit is not for dazzling people with the supernatural, nor is it for someone to build a ministry on that revelation. God gives us the knowledge of the spiritual realm for specific purposes. The ultimate end is always to set captives free and for people to walk in the freedom that has been received.

119

Several years ago, I began to wonder as Gideon did, where are the mighty miracles in our generation that I read about in the Bible? I noted in Judges 2, that if a generation does not see the miraculous supernatural intervention of Almighty God on their behalf, they cannot keep from serving idols. At the end of Judges, it says that everyone did what was right in his own sight. They had no measuring rod by which to judge themselves, and consequently they were a mess.

The catalyst in my own ministry is to see God's people victorious, strong, alive, excited about Jesus, living holy and pure lives. Out of the overflow of Christ and the Holy Spirit, I have been witness to blind eyes seeing, deaf ears hearing, the lame walking, cancers vanishing, and His people set free. I am seeing more souls being born again, and backsliders returning to Jesus. I fully expect it all to continue and increase.

The thing that drives me, is to see myself and God's people in unconditional obedience to the Word, because therein is the only protection and security for our lives. The challenge is to live a life of joyous victory in Jesus wherever you are, whatever you are called to do, and others will want what you have.

An Encounter With Seducing Spirits

Not long ago, I was scheduled to minister and was making the necessary arrangements. If at all possible, I prefer to stay in a non-smoking room because as a non-smoker, the odor of a smoke saturated room is terribly offensive and unhealthy. The motels in the city where I was to stay didn't have non-smoking rooms, however, there was available a "bed and breakfast" that was totally non-smoking. Having stayed in a bed and breakfast in Europe, I knew that they could be very lovely. I was also comfortable in my decision to stay there, even though I knew I would be there alone.

Just before I left for these meetings, I discovered that I was to minister four services on Sunday, one on Monday, and two on Tuesday, and then fly back to Georgia on Wednesday. Before I left to minister, I asked those who I was able to contact, "Please pray for strength of the human body. The anointing will take care of itself." I knew I had a heavy ministry schedule, but what I didn't realize at the time, was that God directed me to put a wall of fire of intercession around me that couldn't be penetrated.

The Saturday I arrived, I was driven to the inn, and as I approached the building, a sense of darkness and hesitancy crept over me. I rationalized, "Well, it's just because the building is so old."

When I entered the building, I was astonished at the surroundings. Never had I seen a more exquisitely decorated inn or hotel. The owners were out of town, but the hostess was extremely gracious. She took me on a tour of the inn, and every room to the most minute detail was just lovely.

The hostess spoke in a peaceful, kind manner as she talked about the decor. She mentioned the owner's name along with "another hand that guided her." When she said that, my spirit jumped and said, "New Age. This place is owned by New Agers." I was then taken to an absolutely beautiful room.

The couple who owned the inn arrived the next day. When I met her, I knew beyond any doubt that they in fact were into the New Age movement. The woman was one who even discipled others in this cult.

From all outward appearances, you could not have asked for a more calm, gracious, and gentle atmosphere.

The environment was impeccably well designed, and they spoke in sweet, gentle tones. They talked about *energy* continuously, but they didn't know the source of all life, God Almighty. There was a surface calm, but all was not as it appeared.

With the exception of one night, I was the only guest in the whole building. The owner couldn't seem to stay away from me. She knew there was a powerful energy in me, but they were in total confusion about this "super-energy." We know that it is the Holy Spirit.

Their "light" was darkness compared to the light that shines from the believer. I was very aware that their energy was being channeled against me. On that Monday, I was on my face weeping by the Spirit of the Lord for their deliverance and salvation.

As I was leaving on Wednesday, they had a most puzzled look on their faces. They were speaking to another man who was a repairman. He had been called to check on the reason for the failure of their subliminal music system into my room. They didn't know it, but during the entire time, I played tape recordings of the Word of God, along with praise and worship tapes on my small cassette player. The power of the Word, praise and worship tapes had totally blocked out the subliminal music designed to affect my soul.

1 JOHN 4:4

4 Ye are of God, little children, and have overcome them: because greater is he that is in you, than he that is in the world.

The purpose of this story is to show the operation of seducing spirits. I was exposed to people who expressed outward kindness, gentleness, peace, and gracious hospitality. It was not by mere coincidence that I spent those days there. It was by divine appointment, to pray for their salvation, but also to learn more about the body of Christ and the image it projects to the world.

Questions began to arise in my own mind. What kind of picture are Christians giving to those with whom we have contact? Are we just moaning and complaining about how bad things look or may get? Are we presenting a God who heals or delivers when He feels like it, contrary to God's Word? Are we portraying a God who tolerates blatant willful sin? Are they seeing long faces, without peace, hope, or joy? Are they hearing a lack of faith, or confidence in the sustaining power of our God? Does our light shine?

What are we giving to the world? People who don't know God will seldom read the Bible just because someone gives it to them. It would take an act of divine grace to prompt a person, searching for truth, to read a Bible in the quest of God. To be sure, that does happen on occasion. However, by and large, people read living epistles, that is, the lives of Christians.

Are we inspiring the unsaved, or are we presenting to them a life that says, "Well, I'm a little confused about it all myself. I really don't understand, but I guess it will all be okay in the sweet bye-and-bye." Most unbelievers at first really don't care about the sweet bye-and-bye. They want answers for their lives in the here and now. They want to experience peace, joy, health, and victory now.

The real challenge for the Christian is to know this Jesus Whom we serve. Can others say of us, as they said of those in the fourth chapter of Acts, that we are noteworthy because we had been with Jesus? How could they tell that they had been with Jesus? Well, Jesus was all over them. He was emanating from their entire being.

Murmuring kept the children of Israel out of the promised land. They refused to believe that the God Who so mightily delivered them out of Egypt, would be with them in overcoming the obstacles in possessing the land. They had a grasshopper mentality. It kept them in the wilderness for 40 years, until that unbelieving generation died off.

God does not withhold from His children. It is disobedience and lack of childlike trust in our Father God, that keeps us from possessing what belongs to us. The God of Abraham is the God of the living and not the dead, and Jesus is truly the same yesterday, today, and forever. He does not withhold good things from those who trust him.

If we didn't know Jesus as we do, the way that New Age thinking is spreading would be frightening. Humanism is the ruling thought in our public institutions. In essence, it says that the answer to all of humanity's problems can be found in the human intellect, will, and use of its resources. In spite of its claims for the betterment of humanity, the fact is that society's problems are growing worse. Humanism didn't work for the people of Nimrod's time (Genesis 10 and 11), and has been a failure throughout the ages. Sadly, the deception continues.

Christians need to know that it is ultimately a spiritual struggle. Whether we know about it or not, we are in a war. We have an active enemy that is seeking to devour all that he is given license to destroy, either by will or by ignorance. However, the good news is that we are not left defenseless or left to our own devices. God has made ample provision for our victory.

Doctrines of Demons

1 TIMOTHY 4:1-3 (Amplified Bible)

1 But the (Holy) Spirit distinctly and expressly declares that in latter times some will turn away from the faith, giving attention to deluding and seducing spirits and doctrines that demons teach,

2 Through the hypocrisy and pretensions of liars whose consciences are seared (cauterized),

3 Who forbid people to marry and [teach them] to abstain from (certain kinds of) foods which God created to be received with thanksgiving by those who believe and have (an increasingly clear) knowledge of the truth.

Whenever there is a situation where the lawful marriage relationship is ignored, or entirely forbidden, the operation of seducing spirits is behind it. When people live together and are not lawfully married according to the law of the land, they are operating under seducing spirits.

God is the one who created the institution of marriage. It is for the safety and protection of the family, to keep it from being broken, and to keep the heritage of the children intact. The devil wants to destroy families and the bonds of unity in marriage.

If you are living with someone and are not married, you have been beguiled by demons. It will end up in destruction, so you need to repent and make it right. Either get married or separate yourself from that situation.

There is also the situation where people are forbidden to marry. There is nothing wrong with someone *choosing* to live a life of celibacy. However, it is a doctrine of devils, when it is imposed. In other words, there are cults wherein celibacy is a requirement, and it is a contingency of spirituality.

Another doctrine of devils is the requirement to abstain from certain kinds of foods that God has given for us to receive with thanksgiving. People can get very religious over food, especially "health food." You can get caught up in the scrutiny of food to the point where it preoccupies your life. We need to be wise and use good judgment in the foods we consume, however, fanaticism is based in fear. That fear is the entrance for seducing spirits.

God has created everything good, and nothing is to be refused if it is received with thanksgiving. It is consecrated by the Word of God. When I pray over my food, He blesses what I eat and what I drink. The Lord removes all sickness and disease, He shall fulfill all the days of my life, and as the days of my life are, so shall my strength be. Now that is the best vitamin tablet you can take!

EXODUS 23:25

25 And ye shall serve the Lord your God, and he shall bless thy bread, and thy water; and I will take sickness away from the midst of thee.

In 1 Timothy 4:1,2, it says that those who forbid marriage and enforce dietary laws, are hypocrites and liars, who have had their consciences cauterized, that is, burned, until no life can penetrate it. It says that these have been seduced away from the faith by evil spirits.

How the Seducing Spirit Operates

The word "seduce" in Greek is *apoplanao*, which means to lead astray in an active sense. The prefix *apo* means "from." The root word *planao* is causative, that is, to cause to stray. Therefore, we can see that the seducing spirit is sent from the seducer, himself.

1 JOHN 2:15,16

15 Love not the world, neither the things that are in the world. If any man love the world, the love of the Father is not in him.

16 For all that is in the world, the lust of the flesh, and the lust of the eyes, and the pride of life, is not of the Father, but is of the world.

Verse 16 tells us the three categories of bait that is used by the seducer. They are lust, greed, and pride. It speaks of believers being lead astray, enticed by the things of this world. It is covetousness, and Ephesians 5:5 equates one who covets with an idolater.

EPHESIANS 5:5

5 For this ye know, that no whoremonger, nor unclean person, nor covetous man, who is an idolater, hath any inheritance in the kingdom of Christ and of God.

An example of a person under the influence of seducing spirits is Absalom, son of King David, who coveted his father's throne. He decided that his father was not running the kingdom of Israel well enough to suit him. He thought he could do a far better job, and decided that he was going to take over his father's kingdom.

2 SAMUEL 15:10

10 But Absalom sent spies throughout all the tribes of Israel, saying, As soon as ye hear the sound of the trumpet, then ye shall say, Absalom reigneth in Hebron.

Seducing spirits work through flattery. They tell you that you are wonderful and that the world just cannot get along without you or your input.

DANIEL 11:32

32 And such as do wickedly against the covenant shall he corrupt by flatteries: but the people that do know their God shall be strong, and do exploits.

If you are obeying God and His Word, the devil can't seduce you. Conversely, the devil will convince you that all the unholy things people do are alright in the eyes of God.

Several years ago, I was ministering in a mid-western state. One evening the pastor shared with me about a situation which greatly troubled him. There was a young couple in his congregation. The young man was born again and Spirit-filled. He was living with his girl-friend, who was unsaved.

In the course of time, she received the Lord, and still continued to live with him. As she began to grow in the Lord, she was convicted of her lifestyle and became very troubled. She told him that they could no longer stay in that situation as it was, because it was wrong.

He responded that their relationship was pure and holy before God and that it was alright to live together even though they were not married. He was deceived by a seducing spirit. She became so confused that she went to the pastor and told him the whole story.

The young man with whom she was living was so deceived, that he perverted God's Word to satisfy his own lust. The young woman told the pastor that after they would have sexual relations, he would turn his face to the wall and quote 1 John 1:9, saying, "If we confess our sins, he is faithful and just to forgive us our sins, and to cleanse us from all unrighteousness."

The pastor called the young man into his office to speak with him about the situation. His response to the pastor's confrontation was, "Pastor, you are bringing me under condemnation. It is written that there is therefore no condemnation to them which are in Christ Jesus."

Do you see how complete the deception was? It's just like the devil to give you part of the truth, and leave the significant piece conveniently out. He never finished the rest of Romans 8:1b, which says, "...who walk not after the flesh, but after the Spirit."

Coup d'etat

In the realm of political life, a coup d'etat is a sudden overthrow of a government that has been plotted by its opponents. It is the kind of thing that Absalom attempted against his father, King David. Seducing spirits are behind these plots.

In February, 1983, I ministered in Guatemala and had the opportunity to speak and minister to the heads of state at the presidential palace. I usually do not go to the same foreign country more than once in the same year, but in June of that year, the Lord spoke to me and said that I would return in July to Guatemala City, back to the presidential palace.

He told me that I was to arrive there on July 6th and have my feet in the presidential palace on July 7th. On July 8th, I was to lead His people in uninterrupted intercession from 5:00 p.m. until midnight. He would then have me out of the country the very next day, July 9th. He also said, "Leave the rest to Me."

At the time God spoke this to me, I was not even seeking Him for anything. I was merely walking to my dressing table, getting myself ready to minister for an evening service. All that He said, however, came to pass.

When I arrived, I was told that reliable believers had prophecies, dreams, and visions that there would be the worst coup d'etat in Guatemala that had ever taken place. It would be a bloodbath, unless it could be averted.

At that time, the president was a Spirit-filled Christian. On the night of July 7th, I was praying in his home with him and another head of state, along with their wives. One wife was writing down what I was speaking in tongues. I was speaking in Spanish, although I do not speak Spanish in the natural. They were receiving from God what to expect and what to pray about.

As I laid my hands on the president in prayer, I had two visions. I saw him behind prison bars, stretching out his right arm. In his right hand, he was holding out a whole loaf of bread. God said, "He is My man, and he is attempting to hold out the bread of life to My people, the people of Guatemala, but he is held in prison and bondage." God then revealed the bondage to me. In another vision, I saw a giant hand swoop down and take a crown from off his head.

I didn't tell a soul about what I had seen. The next day we prayed in the Spirit for seven hours, from 5:00 p.m. until midnight. I had hoped we would avert these two visions by our prayers. One month later to the day, on August 8, 1983, there was a successful coup d'etat and this president was removed from office. These two visions came to pass, however, there was absolutely no bloodshed because that had been averted by the seven hours of intercession.

Almost a year later I received a call from the person who headed up the intercession for Guatemala at that time. He is a Spirit-filled believer who has brought intercession to several Central American nations. He said, "Bobbie Jean, we have finally gotten into a position for God to show us why that happened."

I was very curious about it myself. I wondered why God had sent me to pray for seven hours. Thank God there was no bloodbath, but I really wanted what I had seen in the visions to be averted as well. That is why I didn't want to tell anyone about the visions.

The man said, "We have been seeking God since it happened to tell us where we missed it." He continued, "God has showed us that what we gained in intercession, we did not maintain in intercession." What he was saying is that when we get the victory, we must keep the victory.

Demons are assigned to plot a coup against your nation, church, home, business, health, and whatever belongs to you. They want to take your territory, but you do not have to let them.

Satan is a master strategist. One of his strategies is to keep you busy putting out brush fires and minor skirmishes, while the real battle rages on somewhere else. He wants to keep you cutting things off the top, instead of digging up the root and letting God cast it aside.

How are coups brought about by demons? They accuse the brethren to one another. They seduce the brethren into thinking they are better in some way than their brother. Jesus did not come to condemn, but to save.

Jesus is also calling for justice and righteousness. He has given the five ministry gifts to perfect and equip the saints to do the work of the ministry. According to Hebrews 13, the ministry gifts of apostle, prophet, pastor, evangelist, and teacher, are going to give an accounting to God for the souls of His sheep. It is our souls that those who have the rule over us try to keep straightened out and on the right path.

You may not always like what the ministry gift is doing. Pray for them, instead of rebelling. It is God's authority in the church. He says that there is no authority that has not been given by Him.

When people are accusing and gossiping about others, you can be sure you are next. They flatter you to your face, but soon they are talking about you to somebody else. It is beguiling, seducing spirits at work, causing strife in the body of Christ, in an attempt to stop the work of the ministry.

It is time for holiness and purity in the body of Christ. It is time to recognize the working of unclean spirits and get free so that revival can take place.

Five "R"s in Revival

Revival is a word that has come to mean several things. It is simply the awakening of something that is dead. It can be on an individual level, a church congregational level, or on a national level.

Revelation

The first step is receiving a revelation. Salvation needs to be revealed before a person can respond. It has been my experience that God never reveals something to us until we are ready to make a change. He gives us the revelation of what needs to be removed, and how to do it. He also gives us the grace to do it. His timing is always perfect.

Repentance

Then after revelation, comes repentance, "For godly sorrow worketh repentance..." (2 Corinthians 7:10a). The Greek word for repentance is *metanoeo*. It is the combination of two parts. *Meta* means "after, implying change," and *noeo* means "to perceive". Putting them together gives us the concept of changing one's mind, purpose, or direction. In the New Testament it is always used as a change for the better, a turning away from sin.

Restitution

After repentance comes restitution. There are some things that we have to make right with people. This goes beyond the "I apologize" and "I forgive you." Forgiveness comes with repentance, but restitution is setting things in order, or repaying damages where possible.

Restoration

Unlike forgiveness, restoration takes time. For example, when a marriage is ripped apart due to adultery, there may be instant forgiveness. Restoring the marriage, however, takes some time and effort from both parties until trust and confidence is built up again.

There is always a time factor involved in restoration. God will work in the restoration process, but we must allow patience, long-suffering, kindness, gentleness, and understanding to work in us.

Revival

When revelation, repentance, restitution, and restoration are working, revival is ripe for bursting forth. When things are right within us, the devil can't do anything.

When you give him no place to operate, then the devil has no part in you or what concerns you. He can't find an opening to do his dastardly deeds.

We need to get right with Almighty God, receive His grace, and obey His Word. With that combination at work, the devil has no entry into our lives. He has no power, or dominion because we are walking in the Spirit and the authority of the Word of God in Jesus Name. That is what personal revival is all about.

A coup is usually carried out by military support. It is a militant action carried out by the supporters of the opposition with the objective of removing the current authority. We are an army, warriors that carry out the commission of the Lord, Jesus Christ, our Commander-in-chief. We are advancing against the gates of hell, and they cannot prevail.

Seducing spirits will tell you that you are not making an impact, so don't bother to pray or keep your life pure and holy. The Word of God says, however, that you have authority over the works of darkness and that you are making an impact in the kingdom of God and against the works of darkness. His Word says that you are the light of the world, and through you His kingdom will be established to the ends of the earth.

One evening I was prophesying in Columbus, Ohio. The prophecy involved the revelation of the Lord Jesus Christ as presented in Matthew 16. The Holy Spirit prompted me to say that when we have a personal and experiential, God-given, Holy Ghost revelation of Jesus Christ, the gates of hell do not slow us up or hold us back, but rather we prevail against them.

A good positive confession is not enough, even though they are good to make. They help renew and train your mind to think according to the Word of God. Nevertheless, nothing will replace a personal revelation of Jesus Christ, the Messiah, the Anointed One.

As we know Who He is for us personally and individually, then when we speak the Word as Jesus did against Satan in Matthew 4:1-11, the gates of hell shall not prevail against us. Is it any wonder that the apostle Paul cried, "Oh! That I might know Him!"

Knowledge is not even enough. You can know enough to quote the Bible from Genesis to Revelation, and the gates of hell will bowl you over unless you *know the Savior.*

Remedy for Seducing Spirits

Having knowledge without wisdom for a situation is not enough. Wisdom is applying a selective piece of knowledge that is appropriate for the circumstance. What then, is the answer for the believer, knowing that there are seducing spirits prowling around? The first chapter of Jeremiah gives great wisdom, but know also that God's entire Word is full of direction and wise counsel.

JEREMIAH 1:5

5 Before I formed thee in the belly I knew thee; and before thou camest forth out of the womb I sanctified thee, and I ordained thee a prophet unto the nations.

Even though these words were specifically spoken to Jeremiah, the prophet, know this for yourself as well. You are separated, set apart, consecrated, and appointed for God's purpose and plan. Begin to recognize it and walk in it.

JEREMIAH 1:7,8

7 But the Lord said unto me, Say not, I am a child: for thou shalt go to all that I shall send thee, and whatsoever I command thee thou shalt speak.

8 Be not afraid of their faces: for I am with thee to deliver thee, saith the Lord.

God will use His people to speak His commands and directives. Don't be afraid when you know that the Holy Spirit is leading and that His anointing is upon you.

JEREMIAH 1:10,11

10 See, I have this day set thee over the nations and over the kingdoms, to root out, and to pull down, and to destroy, and to throw down, to build, and to plant.

11 Moreover the word of the Lord came unto me, saying, Jeremiah, what seest thou? And I said, I see a rod of an almond tree.

Seven things are given to do in verse 10. These seven things are to rule, root out, pull down, destroy, throw down, build, and plant. They speak of repentance, restitution, and restoration. These things are sequential. Before things can be made better, the old useless things that cause destruction have to be rooted out and removed. Repentance requires change of direction, and the rest will follow.

Be alert and active to see and hear what the Spirit of the Lord is doing in your life. Listen for the *rhema*, the spoken Word of God to you.

Repentance, restitution, and restoration begin with hearing and obeying the Word of the Lord so that you can experience His glory. Whatever needs to be adjusted or removed from your life as revealed by the Holy Spirit to you requires your obedience out of a deep desire to please God. Disobedience to His Word does not go unnoticed by God, and eventually judgment will surely follow.

JEREMIAH 1:14-16

14 Then the Lord said unto me, Out of the north an evil shall break forth upon all the inhabitants of the land.

15 For, lo, I will call all the families of the kingdoms of the north, saith the Lord; and they shall come, and they shall set every one his throne at the entering of the gates of Jerusalem, and against all the walls thereof round about, and against all the cities of Judah.

16 And I will utter my judgments against them touching all their wickedness, who have forsaken me, and have burned incense unto other gods, and worshipped the works of their own hands.

God does not tolerate idolatry. As we have seen in Ephesians 5:5, those who are covetous are equated with idolaters. God will not share His glory with another, and if we want to experience the glory of God, we cannot permit the lust of this world to enter into our lives.

JEREMIAH 1:18

18 For, behold, I have made thee this day a defenced city, and an iron pillar, and brasen walls against the whole land, against the kings of Judah, against the princes thereof, against the priests thereof, and against the people of the land.

What God said to Jeremiah, He is also saying to you. He gives divine strength, which no hostile power can overcome. Isn't that powerful?

LUKE 21:15 (Amplified Bible)

15 For I [Myself] will give you a mouth and such utterance and wisdom that all of your foes combined will be unable to stand against or refute.

ACTS 6:10 (Amplified Bible)

10 But they were not able to resist the intelligence and the wisdom and [the inspiration of] the Spirit with which he spoke.

JEREMIAH 1:19

19 And they shall fight against thee; but they shall not prevail against thee; for I am with thee, saith the Lord, to deliver thee.

These are the promises of our God. We just need to take Him at His Word. We can rest in Him, knowing that we shall prevail and have victory because our God is with us.

JEREMIAH 5:1 (Amplified Bible)

1 Run to and fro through the streets of Jerusalem, and see now and take notice! Seek in her broad squares to see if you can find a man [as Abraham sought in Sodom], one who does justice, who seeks truth, sincerity and faithfulness; and

I will pardon Jerusalem — for one uncompromisingly righteous person.

Because God does not change, we see that He has always sought to save for the sake of the righteous. We can point to the rise of the New Age philosophies, and perversions taking place in our nation, but for the sake of the righteous, God will save the land. The unrighteous will not take over because of the presence of believers, made righteous by the blood of Jesus.

JEREMIAH 6:10 (Amplified Bible)

10 To whom shall I, Jeremiah, speak and give warning, that they may hear? Behold, their ear is uncircumcised [never brought into covenant with God, or consecrated to His service], and they cannot hear or obey. Behold, the word of the Lord has become to them a reproach and the object of their scorn; they have no delight in it.

This is how to overcome. Have a circumcised ear, that is, an ear that is in covenant with God so that you are consecrated to His service. If you don't have your ear tuned to what God is telling you, you will not be able to obey Him and fulfill what He is calling you to do.

Seducing spirits can't be heard by a consecrated ear that listens only to the voice of God. You can't have that circumcised ear unless you are willing to be obedient to the will of God for your life and are determined to follow in a life of service to Him.

Chapter 7
The Challenge

There are many areas wherein Americans have been the vanguard, setting the pace for the rest of the world. Technology, entertainment, and fashion are just a few. It is therefore, important to know that what happens here, does affect the rest of the world, and therefore, we cannot allow ourselves to become spiritually lethargic.

In Washington, D.C., I ministered this topic of the spirit of python. I explained that it is a triune spirit, that is, python, divination, and religion. It is one and the same spirit, but it functions in three different ways. It also has three companions, which are Jezebel, beguiling, and seducing spirits. Add to these, the controlling and manipulating spirits.

While there, I spoke some advice that is just good daily practice for all believers, and that is to declare the blood of Jesus Christ over themselves.

HEBREWS 9:14
14 How much more shall the blood of Christ, who through the eternal Spirit offered himself without spot to God, purge your conscience from dead works to serve the living God?

Specifically, your head is covered by the blood of Jesus Christ so that no evil thoughts can be planted by the devil and your mind stays focused on Jesus Christ.

Your hands are covered with the blood of Jesus Christ, so that all you put your hands to do will be holy and protected. Your feet are covered by the blood of Jesus Christ, so you can walk in a lifestyle that is led of the Spirit.

Whenever I have ministered on topics concerning the activities of python, which has not been often, pastors have contacted me and told me that I have thoroughly described their situation. They are amazed that I have so specifically revealed what they are going through, and ask, "How do we get the victory? How do we stop the manifestation and administration of that spirit?"

One of the things that the devil would like you to believe is that you are the only one on this planet that is going through a particular hardship. That is a lie that is planted to keep you isolated from the rest of the body of Christ, and struggling alone until you give up. It is all a part of his deception.

The body of Christ has received great teaching on many subjects like intercessory prayer, bombarding the gates of hell, pulling down strongholds. We even have received teachings on praise as an instrument of warfare. Yet people who seem to be applying all that they know are not always experiencing victory and maintaining it.

I searched the Word and I sought the Lord regarding this, and He revealed some things to me. He showed me that the problem is not always in the heavenlies, the ruling spirit of python, or the New Age army. Yes, Satan has an army and we are in a battle. The battle is for the souls of people that are going to hell because of deception by beguiling and seducing spirits.

The Lord revealed that a good part of the problem centers around what is promised in 2 Chronicles 7:14.

2 CHRONICLES 7:14

14 If my people, which are called by my name, shall humble themselves, and pray, and seek my face, and turn from their wicked ways; then will I hear from heaven, and will forgive their sin, and will heal their land.

The first condition mentioned is for God's people to humble themselves. It is something they must do, not something that He will do to them.

Humility is obeying the Word of God unconditionally. It is having an inner attitude of holiness that keeps you right with God. It keeps your attitude, aims, goals, purposes, and motives pure before God.

Yes, we are the righteousness of God in Christ Jesus, and it is not of ourselves but what He has accomplished on our behalf. Good works do not earn the righteousness of God, it was paid for by the work of Calvary for us. However, we are to bear the fruits of righteousness.

Therefore, when God said He would heal our land if we would humble ourselves and pray, He's not just talking about calling a prayer meeting. He's not just talking about people who travail or even do militant praise and warfare. He is talking about people who will find out what He has to say about how they are to live.

Most assuredly, God wants us to pray earnestly and diligently. However, the humbling and praying is connected with "turn from their wicked ways" in the same sentence.

When we get our lives in divine order, submitted to God, there is no power of darkness that can stop us. There is nothing of flesh, including New Age or Satanists, that can stop the blessings of God from happening. Nothing will interfere with bringing in the souls that have the Name of God on their heads for the glory of God, from the North, the South, the East, and the West. (Read Isaiah 43:5-7.)

A diversionary tactic will keep you focused on the wiles of the devil, when your attention should be in cleaning up the body of Christ. The local church needs to be pulled together in divine order and walk in the unity that God wants in the body of Christ. Then nothing will be impossible for you to accomplish what is within the will of God for your life.

People do a lot of casting out of demons, when there is no demon to cast out. It is flesh that needs to die. Demons are not always the cause of wrong things in a person's life. Although that is the case sometimes, I have found this frequently is a case of not wanting repentance, that is, not willing to make the necessary changes to walk in victory.

Herein is the challenge. Yes, we need to continue intercession, to continue praise and worship, and continue in the Word. It is also time to get our lives straight before Almighty God. When we do, the heavens will not be brass, and no demonic force will be able to stand against the advancement of God's army.

Respect for God's Ministers

In 1 Corinthians 5, there was a serious situation in the church at Corinth that Paul was addressing. Someone in the congregation was having an affair with his father's wife. Paul was very distressed over their lack of dealing with this circumstance and he chastised them.

1 CORINTHIANS 5:3-5

3 For I verily, as absent in body, but present in spirit, have judged already, as though I were present, concerning him that hath so done this deed,

4 In the name of our Lord Jesus Christ, when ye are gathered together, and my spirit, with the power of our Lord Jesus Christ,

5 To deliver such an one unto Satan for the destruction of the flesh, that the spirit may be saved in the day of the Lord Jesus.

They were obedient, and Paul wrote them again. In 2 Corinthians 2:9, Paul writes,

2 CORINTHIANS 2:9 (Amplified Bible)

9 For this was my purpose in writing you, to test your attitude and see if you would stand the test, whether you are obedient and altogether agreeable [to following my orders] in everything.

Related to this issue, my husband Milton received a word from the Lord a few years ago. He asked the Lord why numerous ministers have so many mighty miracles occur while ministering in foreign countries, yet do not experience this to the same degree when ministering in the United States.

The Lord responded that we did not have the respect for the apostles, prophets, evangelists, pastors, and teachers, as they do in other countries. We need to respect the authority and the anointing of the office, so that we will receive the edifying and perfecting that is being ministered through them.

Paul was a man that had a good perspective of what he had been, and what Jesus made him, by His call, and His anointing. When he gave a directive, he gave it by the Holy Spirit, and expected it to be carried out.

2 CORINTHIANS 2:10 (Amplified Bible)

10 If you forgive any one anything, I too forgive that one; and what I have forgiven, if I have forgiven anything, has been for your sakes in the presence [and with the approval] of Christ, (the Messiah).

To the natural mind, it sounds like boasting. However, Paul knew who he was, and he also knew Jesus.

Paul finishes by saying, "To keep Satan from getting the advantage over us; for we are not ignorant of his wiles and intentions" (2 Corinthians 2:11, Amplified Bible). Forgiveness means restoration, and renewing love for the person. Paul is saying that if you don't forgive, you are opening the door for Satan. Unforgiveness gives entry to strife.

How Religion, Divination, and Python Work

Satan controls unregenerated man, nations, governments, and empires through religion, divination, and python.

2 CORINTHIANS 4:4-6

4 In whom the god of this world hath blinded the minds of them which believe not, lest the light of the glorious gospel of Christ, who is the image of God, should shine unto them.

5 For we preach not ourselves, but Christ Jesus the Lord; and ourselves your servants for Jesus' sake.

6 For God, who commanded the light to shine out of darkness, hath shined in our hearts, to give the light of the knowledge of the glory of God in the face of Jesus Christ.

Those who believe, do so out of an act of their will. Those who do not believe, have blinders on their eyes. Horses and mules have blinders put on so that they stay on one path and are not able to see another direction. In like manner, unbelievers have blinders to keep them from seeing the alternate direction for their lives, the direction that leads to eternal life.

Unbelievers who have been presented with the truth, are deceived, seduced, and are taking an imitation because they refuse to believe the simple Word of God. Even those who have never heard the gospel preached are blinded by the god of this world and are held in bondage to religions.

Winds of Doctrine

In Ephesians 4:14, the process of deception is described.

EPHESIANS 4:14

14 That we henceforth be no more children, tossed to and fro, and carried about with every wind of doctrine, by the sleight of men, and cunning craftiness, whereby they lie in wait to deceive;

This shows how manipulating spirits work through men. The word "sleight" in Greek is *kubeia*, which denotes dice-playing as used in gambling. It represents trickery, expert manipulation, or being sly.

We can see from this verse, that there is every intent to deceive through manipulation. Erroneous doctrine is the vehicle of entrapment and the goal is to deceive believers away from the faith.

Notice that those who are being deceived are called children. In 1 Corinthians 3:1 and Ephesians 4:14, the words "babes" and "children" in the Greek context, literally mean non-speaking infants. We grow in faith by speaking the Word of God in prayer and confessions of faith. Therefore, there is great impact when we are admonished to avoid being like "non-speaking infants." These are the ones who are easily deceived, not having the ability to speak the Word of God. On the contrary, those who are well grounded and mature in the Word of God are not easily deceived by heresies.

Here is how a wind of doctrine blows around in our day. Someone gets an erroneous tidbit from the enemy by deception, and then writes a book about it. He may even be a very charismatic preacher and sell tapes about his revelation. The unlearned, unsuspecting believer swallows the whole package because it sounds great, or because the person is famous, or better yet, because it's in print. After all, if it's in print, it must be the truth. Right? Wrong!

They have not thoroughly checked it out with the Word of God, nor have they prayed about it and sought the wisdom of the Holy Spirit, Who is the great Teacher of the body of Christ. The next person comes along and refutes that revelation in his book, and the believer is totally confused. When you listen to someone's revelation, even if they are absolutely accurate, you have an obligation as a follower of Christ, to check it out in His Word, and then take it to the prayer closet.

When you go out to a restaurant and order a steak for dinner, the steak belongs to the restaurant. When you cut it, put it into your mouth, and chew it, it ceases to belong to the restaurant. It is then assimilated into your body and that steak is now yours.

The same is true with a revelation of God's Word. It can be set before you, but until you get alone with Almighty God and allow that word to assimilate into you by the Holy Spirit, it will never be yours. Anybody can come along and take it away from you. You counterattack that by the truth of God's Word being ministered to you personally by the Holy Spirit.

Wolves in Sheep's Clothing

The spirit of divination, religion, and python is not obvious about his presence or influence. He is not going to cross your path leading a brass band and wearing a red hat. How does he come? Jesus said, "Beware of false prophets, which come to you in sheep's clothing, but inwardly they are ravening wolves" (Matthew 7:15). He is talking about leaders who are not what they seem to be.

ACTS 20:28-32

28 Take heed therefore unto yourselves, and to all the flock, over the which the Holy Ghost hath made you overseers, to feed the church of God, which he hath purchased with his own blood.

29 For I know this, that after my departing shall grievous wolves enter in among you, not sparing the flock.

30 Also of your own selves shall men arise, speaking perverse things, to draw away disciples after them.

31 Therefore watch, and remember, that by the space of three years I ceased not to warn every one night and day with tears.

32 And now, brethren, I commend you to God, and to the word of his grace, which is able to build you up, and to give you an inheritance among all them which are sanctified.

Paul, under the inspiration of the Holy Spirit, was admonishing pastors to be alert and on guard because there are those who come to the local church with the purpose of tearing the sheep apart. Not only that, but there can also be those who will rise up within the congregation, who will try to pull others to themselves and cause factions and divisions.

In June, 1986, I had a significant dream concerning this. In this dream, I was looking out from my grandmother's back porch. The events of the dream were happening on the left side of the road where there was a beautiful garden that my grandmother always kept.

Little sheep were frolicking and having a marvelous time. I then saw Jesus descending upon the sheep. When His feet touched the very top of the sheep, they instantly lined up in rows of five.

One gray colored sheep said, "I'm not going to line up with the others. I'm going to keep on playing. I just want to do my own thing." He went on kicking up his little heels. Suddenly, I noticed a wolf disguised as a sheep coming to devour the rebellious sheep who refused to get into divine order.

God's word to me from that dream was, "I'm bringing my church into divine order. It's going to start with the leaders, the five ministry gifts, and consequently, the body of Christ will line up right behind them. The ones that don't line up are going to be susceptible to the ravening wolf." You see, you are not safe out there alone, or without scriptural, godly order.

Have you ever met someone who was so sweet and pleasant, but something down on the inside told you that everything was just not right. If you stay with them long enough, you will find out that they just wanted to devour you.

EZEKIEL 22:25 (Amplified Bible)

25 There is a conspiracy of [Israel's false] prophets in the midst of her, like a roaring lion tearing the prey; they have devoured human lives; they have taken [in their greed] treasure and precious things; they have made many widows in the midst of her.

This is a warning to those who believe. Who are the false prophets? Don't believe everybody that says, "Thus saith the Lord...", or "In the Name of the Lord,...."

There is an amusing story about a man who was supposedly prophesying in a service, in which he mentioned something about Moses' ark. He kept on for a while, and then abruptly said, "Wait just a minute folks. The Lord made a mistake. It wasn't Moses' ark, it was Noah's ark." Then he went right on with what he was saying.

The story may be comical, but the message is that sometimes people speak by the flesh and not by the Spirit of God. You must be alert. You must know God's Word and His will for you. You can't believe everyone who says, "Thus saith the Lord." Be kind to them, but if it doesn't bear witness with your spirit, just love them, pray for them, and put their words on a shelf. If you know it is error, just throw it out.

God is drawing a line and you will have to decide on which side you will stand. He is cleansing the body of Christ and requiring that we stand in faith pleasing Him.

Ezekiel 22:26 describes a corrupt priesthood, one in which the leadership has become as wolves in sheep's clothing.

EZEKIEL 22:26

26 Her priests have violated my law, and have profaned mine holy things: they have put no difference between the holy and profane, neither have they shewed difference between the unclean and the clean, and have hid their eyes from my sabbaths, and I am profaned among them.

The Holy Spirit is moving us from dependency on human beings, to total trust and dependency on Almighty God, Who purchased us by the blood of Jesus Christ.

Ministers are obligated by the grace of God to teach the difference between good and evil. They have the responsibility to present before God's people, that which is holy and that which is unholy. Rebuke and reproof are part of that message. It has to work in their own lives as well, because ministers are also sheep.

There must also be a covering of love and compassion, which motivates a message of correction. It comes from a heart that wants to spare the sheep from harm. It must be done in the grace of God. Ezekiel 22:27-30 continues on in the same vein.

EZEKIEL 22:27-30

27 Her princes in the midst thereof are like wolves ravening the prey, to shed blood, and to destroy souls, to get dishonest gain.

28 And her prophets have daubed them with untempered mortar, seeing vanity, and divining lies unto them, saying, Thus saith the Lord God, when the Lord hath not spoken.

29 The people of the land have used oppression, and exercised robbery, and have vexed the poor and needy: yea, they have oppressed the stranger wrongfully.

30 And I sought for a man among them, that should make up the hedge, and stand in the gap before me for the land, that I should not destroy it: but I found none.

There are false prophets that have devoured human lives. Out of their greed, they have taken in the treasure and precious things. God is simply telling us to be alert. He has given us the symptoms. How will we recognize false prophets? Jesus said, "Ye shall know them by their fruits..." (Matthew 7:16a).

Chapter 8
Divination and False Prophets

Examining the fruit of the lives of those who minister in the prophetic office has to do with the fruit of the Spirit in Galatians 5:22 as with all believers. However, the fruit also has to do with what happens to the lives of the people as a result of that ministry. Are they edified and equipped according to Ephesians 4:12? Is there lasting fruit in the lives of these people?

Many years ago, I was employed by a company whose owner only came once a week to the office where I worked. On one of those occasions, he brought his cousin along, and they were both in the office for the day. After six hours passed, I remarked to the owner, "Your cousin is a nice man."

He responded, "Anybody can be nice for six hours. Live with them for six months, and then you will find out what they are really like." Even though the point he made was obviously secular in thought, the principle was true.

Likewise, on the basis of casual exposure, a minister can sound wonderful. Nevertheless, we should be looking for a track record of lasting fruit in his or her ministry.

I JOHN 4:6

6 We are of God: he that knoweth God heareth us; he that is not of God heareth not us. Hereby know we the spirit of truth, and the spirit of error.

151

This verse tells us that truth and error are spiritually motivated. The fruit will determine which spirit is doing the motivating.

2 JOHN 7-9 (Amplified Bible)

7 For many imposters — seducers, deceivers and false leaders — have gone out into the world, men who will not acknowledge (confess, admit) the coming of Jesus Christ, the Messiah, in bodily form; such a one is the imposter — the seducer, the deceiver, the false leader, the antagonist of Christ — and the Antichrist.

8 — Take care; look to yourselves that you may not lose (throw away or destroy) all that we and you have labored for, but that you may [persevere until you] win and receive back a perfect reward — in full.

9 Any one who runs on ahead [of God] and does not abide in the doctrine of Christ — who is not content with what He taught — does not have God; but he who continues to live in the doctrine (teaching) of Christ — does have God; he has both the Father and the Son.

There are many deceivers and spirits of antichrist inspiring their followers. They are trying to nullify the effectiveness of believers, but here is the point. There is a danger signal that shows when deceiving spirits are in operation.

Someone who is launching out ahead of God is not abiding in the doctrine of Christ. He is not living by faith. This is not a person you would want to connect with in ministry. Decisions made by this person are sure to be in the flesh.

God has times and seasons that He wants us to follow. If He is preparing the way and ordering our steps, then we must follow the rhythm of His guidance. When we get off the beat, we get into trouble.

Running ahead of God is yielding to deceiving spirits who have only one goal, and that is to abort the plan of God for your life. If they can get you to dash headlong out from the plan and direction of Almighty God, they will stall the fulfillment of what God has for you.

Simplicity in Christ

2 CORINTHIANS 11:3

3 But I fear, lest by any means, as the serpent beguiled Eve through his subtilty, so your minds should be corrupted from the simplicity that is in Christ.

The serpent was not blatant in his deception plan. It was through subtle suggestion and complication of God's directives. God's ways are simple and clear. You don't have to be a rocket scientist to understand God's love, grace, mercy, and gift of Jesus.

The gospel is a simple message that is designed to reach all of humanity. Anyone who tries to complicate it is operating under the influence of religious spirits.

Spirit of Antichrist

Jesus encountered religious people throughout His earthly ministry. He warned his disciples about deceivers who will claim to be a messiah.

MATTHEW 24:4,5

4 And Jesus answered and said unto them, Take heed that no man deceive you.

5 For many shall come in my name, saying, I am Christ; and shall deceive many.

Seducers will try to draw you into private meetings and secret places, claiming to point you to the messiah. Prophets of darkness will even disguise themselves as workers of miracles for the good of humanity. It will take keen discernment by the grace of the Holy Spirit and the Word of God to be able to distinguish the true prophet of God from the counterfeit.

MATTHEW 24:23,24

23 Then if any man shall say unto you, Lo, here is Christ, or there; believe it not.

24 For there shall arise false Christs, and false prophets, and shall shew great signs and wonders; insomuch that, if it were possible, they shall deceive the very elect.

In these verses, Jesus is telling us that there will be *many* who will try to imitate His works, declaring themselves to be the Messiah. Be alert and not deceived, because they come in disguise saying that they come in the Name of Jesus. In these days, we will have to rely entirely on the Word of God and the Holy Spirit for wisdom to discern the hearts and intents of men. Our natural mental perception is not enough.

1 JOHN 2:18 (Amplified Bible)

18 Boys (lads), it is the last time — hour [the end of this age]. And as you have heard that Antichrist [he who will oppose Christ in the guise of Christ] is coming, even now many antichrists have arisen, which confirms our belief that it is the final (the end) time.

The spirit of antichrist was in manifestation during the time of the first century Church. Many people associate the spirit of antichrist with *Revelation* themes of the future, and don't think of him being actively against the Church since its inception. First John 4:3 makes it very clear, that this spirit has been attacking the revelation of Jesus as the incarnate Son of God from the very beginning.

1 JOHN 4:3

3 And every spirit that confesseth not that Jesus Christ is come in the flesh is not of God: and this is that spirit of antichrist, whereof ye have heard that it should come; and even now already is it in the world.

The goal of this spirit is to discredit and defame the Name of Jesus and destroy the confidence in the power of that Name. It is character assassination at its best. The spirit of antichrist says that Jesus was not really the Son of God and that His Name has no power. Contrary to God's Word, the spirit of antichrist, through the facade of religious belief, denys the miraculous incarnation of Jesus, the accomplished work on Calvary, and the bodily resurrection of Jesus. In essence, it is the denial of the very central truths of Christianity.

JOHN 10:10

10 The thief cometh not, but for to steal, and to kill, and to destroy: I am come that they might have life, and that they might have it more abundantly.

The devil has not changed since these words were first penned. He still is prowling about seeking to destroy whoever he can. He is seeking to exalt himself above Almighty God. Jesus, on the other hand, has come to give us abundant life, filled with hope and victory.

On Trial

In Genesis 44:15, Joseph was speaking to his brothers, saying that he had the ability to "divine", that is, to make a judgment as in a trial.

GENESIS 44:15

15 And Joseph said unto them, What deed is this that ye have done? wot ye not that such a man as I can certainly divine?

"Divine" in Hebrew is *nachash*, meaning to prognosticate. It is also defined as "making trial" as in the situation with Joseph and his brothers, when Joseph's cup was found in Benjamin's sack.

When divination is working against you, there will be a challenge to what you believe, and the judgments you make based on those beliefs. What you stand for will be on trial.

In Genesis 3:5, the devil tried to convince Eve that she could be as gods.

GENESIS 3:5

5 For God doth know that in the day ye eat thereof, then your eyes shall be opened, and ye shall be as gods, knowing good and evil.

She was already created in the image of God. The devil was lying to her. She exchanged her royal mantle of glory for a common fig leaf. The result was death. If you go to that which is not of God, it will produce death in you.

Divination Brings Defilement

When you listen to people who are not giving you godly counsel, there is something that feels wrong, even when everything adds up and is seemingly right.

Diviners are prognosticators who tap into ungodly knowledge and wisdom. They include New Age promoters, astrologers, palm readers, card readers, spiritualists, and numerologists, just to name a few. In an effort to legitimize their work, they now call themselves *readers* instead of fortune tellers. Modern terminology does not soften their ultimate impact. It is a deadly practice and only brings forth ultimate destruction.

God's Law Regarding Divination

DEUTERONOMY 18:9-12

9 When thou art come into the land which the Lord thy God giveth thee, thou shalt not learn to do after the abominations of those nations.

10 There shall not be found among you any one that maketh his son or his daughter to pass through the fire, or that useth divination, or an observer of times, or an enchanter, or a witch.

11 Or a charmer, or a consulter with familiar spirits, or a wizard, or a necromancer.

12 For all that do these things are an abomination unto the Lord: and because of these abominations the Lord thy God doth drive them out from before thee.

God's Word is abundantly clear about unacceptable supernatural practices. Seeking advice from occult practitioners is equivalent to idolatry. This includes New Age "channeling." It is trusting in other gods rather than the Most High God.

DEUTERONOMY 18:13,14

13 Thou shalt be perfect with the Lord thy God.

14 For these nations, which thou shalt possess, hearkened unto observers of times, and unto diviners: but as for thee, the Lord thy God hath not suffered thee so to do.

There are still those who observe and interpret astrological charts, and attempt to give meaning and direction to individuals based on their study. It is still idolatry and an abomination before God.

DEUTERONOMY 18:15-22

15 The Lord thy God will raise up unto thee a Prophet from the midst of thee, of thy brethren, like unto me; unto him ye shall hearken;

16 According to all that thou desiredst of the Lord thy God in Horeb in the day of the assembly, saying, Let me not hear again the voice of the Lord my God, neither let me see this great fire any more, that I die not.

17 And the Lord said unto me, They have well spoken that which they have spoken.

18 I will raise them up a Prophet from among their brethren, like unto thee, and will put my words in his mouth; and he shall speak unto them all that I shall command him.

19 And it shall come to pass, that whosoever will not hearken unto my words which he shall speak in my name, I will require it of him.

20 But the prophet, which shall presume to speak a word in my name, which I have not commanded him to speak, or that shall speak in the name of other gods, even that prophet shall die.

21 And if thou say in thine heart, How shall we know the word which the Lord hath not spoken?

22 When a prophet speaketh in the name of the Lord, if the thing follow not, nor come to pass, that is the thing which the Lord hath not spoken, but the prophet hath spoken it presumptuously: thou shalt not be afraid of him.

God has spoken to His people through prophets at various times and for various reasons. He is clearly saying in these verses that He intends to continue. As believers in Jesus, we have direct access to the Father through prayer and His Word. We can as individuals hear the direct Word of the Lord. However, God still uses prophets to speak forth His assessments and directives. Deuteronomy 18:22 gives good advice concerning how to tell the difference between a prophet of God and a false prophet.

LEVITICUS 18:27-30

27 (For all these abominations have the men of the land done, which were before you, and the land is defiled;)

28 That the land spue not you out also, when ye defile it, as it spued out the nations that were before you.

29 For whosoever shall commit any of these abominations, even the souls that commit them shall be cut off from among their people.

30 Therefore shall ye keep mine ordinance, that ye commit not any one of these abominable customs, which were committed before you, and that ye defile not yourselves therein: I am the Lord your God.

Notice particularly the words "land," "abominable customs," and "cut off." When abominable customs are practiced, the land becomes polluted. This includes the less than obvious practices that amount to idolatry. Collecting objects related to the occult or idolatry may seem harmless, but they are not.

Dragons, crystals, unicorns, carvings of Buddha or other objects that are venerated, draw demonic activity to your home. They may be beautiful and expensive, but ultimately they pollute the land and the home. Such objects should be destroyed. Nevertheless, there is only one place for an idol, and that is in a garbage can after a hammer has been dutifully applied to it. You shouldn't even give it away because you would not want to pollute someone else.

DEUTERONOMY 12:29-32

29 When the Lord thy God shall cut off the nations from before thee, whither thou goest to possess them, and thou succeedest them, and dwellest in their land;

30 Take heed to thyself that thou be not snared by following them, after that they be destroyed from before thee; and that thou enquire not after their gods, saying, How did these nations serve their gods? even so will I do likewise.

31 Thou shalt not do so unto the Lord thy God: for every abomination to the Lord, which he hateth, have they done unto their gods; for even their sons and their daughters they have burnt in the fire to their gods.

32 What thing soever I command you, observe to do it: thou shalt not add thereto, nor diminish from it.

The Canaanites were particularly gruesome in their idolatry and they committed every vile deed imaginable unto their gods. Even if their worship of idols was mild mannered, the directive of God would be the same.

He told them to keep away from such things, and not to even be curious about it. God was directing the nation of Israel to keep their worship of Him pure. It was ultimately for their own protection and the preservation of the land. We know from history that they did not obey God, and it resulted in cycles of idolatry, desolation, repentance, and restoration.

Abominable practices and customs have become very acceptable in our own country. Astrological signs and horoscopes are as common as sliced bread. Medallions and amulets like horns, crystals, ankhs, eyes, and filigree hands, are worn as jewelry by millions of people in this country. It is all superstitious claptrap surreptitiously planted by the devil. It is designed to keep people dependent on other things rather than on Almighty God for their protection and provision.

NUMBERS 22:7

22 And the elders of Moab and the elders of Midian departed with the rewards of divination in their hand; and they came unto Balaam, and spake unto him the words of Balak.

Profit is a powerful motive in the realm of divination. Prognosticators offer words of flattery in exchange for money. They'll tell you just what you want to hear for a fee, and to keep you coming for more.

Flattery and manipulation are twins, and can be found at work in church settings as well. They may sound something like this, "Why are you just sitting in a pew? They are not being fair to you. You should at least be leading intercession. Oh, you are so good, why aren't they letting you preach? You do such a good job sharing the Word, why don't they let you teach? If I were you, I wouldn't stay in this church. I would go where they would let you preach." This kind of talk will cause nothing but destruction.

False Prophets

ISAIAH 44:24-26

24 Thus saith the Lord, thy redeemer, and he that formed thee from the womb, I am the Lord that maketh all things;

> that stretcheth forth the heavens alone; that spreadeth
> abroad the earth by myself;
>
> 25 That frustrateth the tokens of the liars, and maketh
> diviners mad; that turneth wise men backward, and maketh
> their knowledge foolish;
>
> 26 That confirmeth the word of his servant, and performeth
> the counsel of his messengers; that saith to Jerusalem, Thou
> shalt be inhabited; and to the cities of Judah, Ye shall be
> built, and I will raise up the decayed places thereof.

Madness, insanity, oppression, mental depression, anger, hatred, resentment, and bitterness have a partnership with divination. There are prophets who speak forth the Word of God in righteousness with accuracy, and there are also false prophets who do not.

It is dangerous to let people whose ministry is unknown to you prophesy over you and lay hands on you. One of the methods of transference of spirits is through touch. An important reason for having a pastor is so that he or she can protect you from charlatans. Even more importantly, you have the blood and the Name of Jesus for your protection.

Divination was at work in the early rain and most assuredly it is working in the latter rain. More and more we will see an increase in false prophesying, false visions and dreams, and all of the effects that go with it.

JEREMIAH 29:8,9

> 8 For thus saith the Lord of hosts, the God of Israel; Let not
> your prophets and your diviners, that be in the midst of you,
> deceive you, neither hearken to your dreams which ye cause
> to be dreamed.
>
> 9 For they prophesy falsely unto you in my name: I have
> not sent them, saith the Lord.

More than ever, I am convinced that the body of Christ must know the written Word of God. No matter who prophesies, if it contradicts the Word of God, it is false. God's Word is the unchangeable measure of truth, and it validates or refutes all else.

False prophets want to remove you from the land and drive you out so that you will perish. One of the ways that divination operates is to take what has not been earned. Someone comes into the church, and before you know it, there are private whisperings causing people to become dissatisfied.

This spirit causes divisions and factions. Soon that person is drawing sheep unto himself and if allowed to continue, will cause the congregation to splinter off into another church. The pastor builds the work, and someone comes along to take over or pull people away.

Idolatry is the sin of setting your mind against God. An idolater is a slave to the depraved ideas represented by his idol. There is manipulation and control whenever divination, seducing spirits, and the spirit of python is involved. Diviners make their followers fearful and dependent. Their followers believe that something bad will happen to them if they don't stay faithful.

GALATIANS 4:8,9

8 Howbeit then, when ye knew not God, ye did service unto them which by nature are no gods.

9 But now, after that ye have known God, or rather are known of God, how turn ye again to the weak and beggarly elements, whereunto ye desire again to be in bondage?

TITUS 3:3

3 For we ourselves also were sometimes foolish, disobedient, deceived, serving divers lusts and pleasures, living in malice and envy, hateful, and hating one another.

Idolatry takes you from one lust to another. This is the fate of the unsaved, but it does not have to be the story for those who have received the Lord Jesus Christ. Jesus has set us free from that bondage.

We must guard our hearts and be firmly rooted in the Word of God so that we will not be deceived. God is a loving God, Who has given us ample direction, guidance, warning, and grace. Victory over the demonic world is achieved by walking *with Jesus*, one day and one step at a time.

Chapter 9
Winning the War

The compassion of the Holy Spirit within me, combined with the call and anointing upon me, compels me with a desire to see God's people walking in total liberty. It gives me great joy to see God's people experiencing Him for themselves, and not depending on others to tell them about God's nature.

As I travel to churches across the country and abroad for ministry, I speak to many people. They ask, "How can we overcome? What can we do to destroy the works of the spirit of python, divination, and religion, and keep the victory?"

I diligently sought the Lord in prayer about this very issue. I know that there is excellent teaching on prayer, praise, and worship available to the body of Christ. Yet, I felt that there was something else that needed to be brought out by the direction of the Holy Spirit.

Prayer does works. When you diligently seek the Lord about a matter, He answers prayer. God was faithful to reveal some things about the current condition of the church, and some things to come.

Because of my ministry travel abroad, I have been privileged to see large scale revival in Europe and Africa. In July, 1984, I traveled to Birmingham, England with another ministry for a series of meetings. I was asked to teach and lead intercessory prayer for these services.

The number in attendance was reported to be between 2,000 and 3,000 people.

Four years later, in July, 1988, I attended another series of services with another ministry in the same location. This time the number of people had increased to over 20,000. When we are obedient to sow seed, God will bring the increase in His perfect time.

On a national level, I travel across this country to many states as God directs, and there are pockets of revival in various places. By revival, I mean a move of God where no devil, New Age, satanist, or religion could stop the move of God. It's the kind of move that is so anointed, that unsaved people stop believers in supermarkets and elevators to find out about the God they serve.

The Lord showed me that at first, the revival would not occur in massive crusades here like in other countries. It would happen through individuals going about their routines of life. There will be such expressions of joy, peace, righteousness, and the holiness of Almighty God on His people, that others will stop them to inquire how they might be saved.

A well known evangelist once went into a small store, and a man said to him, "I see Jesus Christ in your eyes." The evangelist wanted to know what the man really saw, so he asked the Lord.

The Lord answered him and said, "Well, I live inside of you. I can look out of your eyes if I want to."

Jesus is going to be so evident in us that others will want to come to Christ because they see Him in us. It will happen as believers submit wholeheartedly to the Will of God.

There are those in the body of Christ that are weary and disillusioned. Some have even begun to wonder if

God is real. They are fed up with the politics and other ungodly things that have crept into the church. They are ready for the pure gospel of hope, and a fresh move of the Holy Spirit.

The church in the local body is going to get itself right with Almighty God. There will be a new awareness of purity and commitment to holiness. There will be a new zeal for the house of the Lord that will hate evil and focus on being obedient to the Will of God.

The gates of hell will not prevail against this church. Notable miracles will happen at the hands of these believers. Of this church they will say, "Here they come. They are turning the world upside down."

"I don't want to play church," has been said so often recently, that it has become a cliche. Nevertheless, it expresses the sentiment of so many that have a heart crying out for the reality of a move of the Holy Spirit. There is a sincere desire for revival with the wisdom and stability of Almighty God.

1992, A Critical Year

In prayer, the Lord revealed to me that 1992 would be a critical year for revival. It will hinge on us being faithful and obedient to let the fire of the Holy Spirit cleanse us, as we continue steadfastly to follow the Word of God.

On a return trip from Israel in October, 1988, we stopped over in Brussels, Belgium. My son, John, purchased a newspaper which was filled with articles about projections of European politics and economics. They focused on the year 1992, and the expectations of European nations. It predicted a one money system, and a functional unification of the countries comparable to the states of the U.S.A., with Brussels as a key location.

I do not claim to be an expert on eschatology (study of end times), but it seems obvious that things are lining up for the return of the Lord Jesus Christ. It is encouraging to know that God knew us before the foundations of the world were laid, and He knew we would be alive in this hour. It should give us confidence to know that we were born for this season and time.

The great faith heroes and heroines were people just like you and I, and they must have perceived themselves as you and I perceive ourselves. This is the secret and victory of the ages, to know that in ourselves we are nothing and can do nothing. However, we can be open vessels for God to pour in His glory, power, strength, sufficiency, and ability for His use.

Bible greats like David, Paul, Deborah, and Jael were no more or less human than any one of us. That is why God has directed us to meditate on His Word continuously.

JOSHUA 1:8

8 This book of the law shall not depart out of thy mouth; but thou shalt meditate therein day and night, that thou mayest observe to do according to all that is written therein: for then thou shalt make thy way prosperous, and then thou shalt have good success.

God has also directed us to strengthen one another. Hebrews 10:25 clearly directs us to keep from being isolated. We receive life, light, and love from one another as Jesus is ministered.

HEBREWS 10:25

25 Not forsaking the assembling of ourselves together, as the manner of some is; but exhorting one another: and so much the more, as ye see the day approaching.

Warfare

God is encouraging us, as He spoke prophetically through me in Washington, D.C., in 1988, "Without Me, you can do nothing; but with Me, you can do all things through the strength of the Lord Jesus Christ, who constantly infuses you with the strength of Almighty God. Be strengthened with all might by My Spirit in your inner man. It is not by might; it is not by power, but it is by my Spirit, saith the Lord of warfare, the Lord of armies, the Lord of hosts, Himself."

War has been declared on the occult, the lies of the devil, divination, the spirit of python, and false religion. Exodus 15:3 says, "The Lord is a man of war: the Lord is his name."

God uses the Gideons of this earth in the war. Just consider the possibilities. The Holy Spirit clothes Himself upon you, and turns you into that mighty man or woman of valor, strength, power, and wisdom, just like He did upon Gideon. Even if your family tree is not socially acceptable, or you were born and raised somewhere less than desirable, the Holy Spirit will make you a supernatural hero to the glory of Almighty God.

Even though we have neglected areas that should have been set in order, such as receiving correction for error, God is still willing to help us set these areas straight. He still responds to those who desire His plans and purposes to be accomplished in their lives.

We can say, with an attitude like the woman with the issue of blood, "I am going to press through the crowd, the opposition, and the obstacles. I am going to press through until I touch the hem of His garment, so that His virtue and power may flow through me, and I will be made whole in spirit, soul and body. I will be filled with power so that I can declare the wonders of the

Lord Jesus Christ and turn my upside down world right side up."

Overcoming in the Midst of Trials

The fourth chapter of Acts gives an example of overcoming religious spirits that want to snuff out the liberating message of the gospel. Peter and John were preaching the good news of salvation and signs followed, specifically the healing of the lame man.

The religious hierarchy was upset when 5,000 people responded to the gospel. Peter and John were brought before the high priest and his colleagues for judgment. Peter spoke under the anointing of the Holy Spirit, boldly declaring Who Jesus is, and the message of salvation through His Name. The leaders were astounded by the boldness and clarity with which Peter and John proclaimed the good news.

ACTS 4:13

13 Now when they saw the boldness of Peter and John, and perceived that they were unlearned and ignorant men, they marvelled; and they took knowledge of them, that they had been with Jesus.

These two men were not privileged to have been raised in the finest homes of Jerusalem, with refinement and education. They were ordinary fisherman, but they had the extraordinary Holy Spirit.

The religious leaders could not deny the miracle that had taken place, nor could they refute the wisdom that was preached. They could only resort to threatening the apostles and warning them not to preach in the Name of Jesus.

ACTS 4:21

21 So when they had further threatened them, they let them go, finding nothing how they might punish them, because

of the people: for all men glorified God for that which was done.

Finding themselves powerless to do anything more, the religious leaders released Peter and John. As far as Peter and John were concerned, it was a time for rejoicing that they were counted worthy to have been persecuted for the Name of Jesus. The religious leaders of Peter's day resorted to threatening Peter and John because they realized the impact the apostles were having on the population. These leaders wanted to stop the gospel from spreading. They also had both the authority and power to carry out their threats, which underscores Peter and John's commitment to continue the work of God in the face of adversity and in spite of persecution.

Threats are still being hurled at individuals in the body of Christ as a weapon to stop the move of God. We have the Word of God and the example of our forefathers to follow.

ACTS 4:29-31

29 And now, Lord, behold their threatenings: and grant unto thy servants, that with all boldness they may speak thy word,

30 By stretching forth thine hand to heal; and that signs and wonders may be done by the name of thy holy child Jesus.

31 And when they had prayed, the place was shaken where they were assembled together; and they were all filled with the Holy Ghost, and they spake the word of God with boldness.

How long has it been since you have had a rejoicing party because you were counted worthy to be persecuted for the Name of Jesus? Instead of murmuring and complaining to one another, we ought to have a count-it-all-joy party. As a believer living in a body of flesh, you will encounter temptations, trials, and tests of various kinds. How we respond to these things is vital to our well being.

If you have determined that the trial is persecution for Jesus' Name sake, it is time for rejoicing. When you are able to count yourself worthy to suffer persecution for Jesus, you are doing something that has eternal impact and value. It is time for a count-it-all-joy party, because the victory most assuredly is yours.

1 PETER 4:12-16 (Amplified Bible)

12 Beloved, do not be amazed and bewildered at the fiery ordeal which is taking place to test your quality, as though something strange — unusual and alien to you and your position — were befalling you.

13 But in so far as you are sharing Christ's sufferings, rejoice, so that when His glory (full of radiance and splendor) is revealed you may also rejoice with triumph — exultantly.

14 If you are censured and suffer abuse [because you bear] the name of Christ, blessed [are you] — happy, fortunate, to be envied, with life-joy, and satisfaction in God's favor and salvation, regardless of your outward condition — because the Spirit of glory, the Spirit of God, is resting upon you. On their part He is blasphemed, but on your part He is glorified.

15 But let none of you suffer as a murderer, or a thief, or any sort of criminal, or as a mischief-maker (a meddler) in the affairs of others — infringing on their rights.

16 But if [one is ill-treated and suffers] as a Christian [which he is contemptuously called], let him not be ashamed, but give glory to God that he is [deemed worthy to suffer] in this name.

Begin your count-it-all-joy party by proclaiming the goodness of God. Tell of His magnificence and about how He is El Elyon, the Most High God. Speak of His great and mighty deeds on your behalf. Magnify His Name when you are alone and in the congregation. Exalt His Name, that He is a covenant keeping God, and that His throne is exalted above all others. Declare that Jesus is the King of kings, and the Lord of lords.

Whenever your attitude is right and you speak in agreement with His Word, He hears from heaven and responds. He heals the sick through your hands, or shadow, or handkerchief. He sets the captives free from demons at the command of your words spoken in the Name of Jesus. Signs, wonders, and miracles will flow at the ministering of His Word.

God is helping the church focus back on Jesus, the hope of glory. He is restoring the expectation of God to move and demonstrate the resurrection power of the Lord Jesus Christ in our presence. It is His desire that Philippians 1:20 become manifested reality in His people.

PHILIPPIANS 1:20

20 According to my earnest expectation and my hope, that in nothing I shall be ashamed, but that with all boldness, as always, so now also Christ shall be magnified in my body, whether it be by life, or by death.

As I ministered on this subject in Washington, D.C., in December, 1988, I gave the following prophecy under the inspiration of the Holy Spirit.

I am coming for such a day, and I am coming for such an hour, that will show forth My power. It has been correctly spoken that it will not be just in the power of the Holy Spirit, but it will be in the character of the Holy Spirit. It will be through a people who are pure and holy. It will be through a people who know their infirmities, weaknesses, frailties, and inabilities. It will be a people who have learned and are willing to lay aside all earthly ambition and all that is of pride.

They have one aim, attitude and purpose, that being the Spirit of the Lord Jesus Christ, Himself. They will be able and willing to put on the new man, clothed in righteousness, robed in holiness, clothed in the garments of praise, thanksgiving, and worship. The new man that covers self.

The new man that is willing to seek no glory for their self, but the glory for Almighty God.

I'm bringing together teams in many places, workers who will work together, pull together, bind together, and who will stay together. Such unity has been imitated. Such unity has been attempted in the world system, but I am appearing upon the scene, saith God, through a holy people. By My right arm and by My right hand they shall be stabilized. They shall be established in the position that I have for them. There will be a team spirit of oneness in goal, vision, and purpose. The goal will be the glory for Almighty God, that none shall be glorified but Him alone.

There will be a new awakening in the body as the bride. No, I'll not allow that which I spoke by My Spirit (that in the decade of the '80s there should be coming together the Word and the Spirit, that the world would see a demonstration and a manifestation, yea, even an explosion of the Word and the Spirit together, such as it never had before) to fall to the ground. It is happening already, saith God. There are people that have found the Word to be true.

Most of them have not even heard the Word like many of you. It is in the highways. It's in the hedges. It's where the rejects (as the sophisticated world thinks of them), the little man, the salt of the earth doth live. They are falling upon their faces. They are laying prostrate before Me not ashamed, and they are crying out. They have surrendered all. They have given all. Some have even been imprisoned for their belief and for My power that is manifest upon them.

There shall be an increase for the nation, this nation. As I did not allow My Will not to be done in the recent election, so I will not allow My Will to go undone in the years to come in your nation. As always, I've had a witness in the earth. Some of humanity think that it's a favor unto Me that they enter into the new birth, that they give themselves to Me, and they begin to see all My glory manifested. They think they are doing me a favor. No, it is a privilege designed for them. It is part of My plan.

The American Church

As never before, God is making apparent the distinction between the church and the heathens in our nation. God's nature and attributes are immutable, that is, they do not change. Therefore, those things that were abominable to Him in ancient days have not changed. God does not tolerate sin, but He loves the sinner.

JOHN 3:16

16 For God so loved the world, that he gave his only begotten Son, that whosoever believeth in him should not perish, but have everlasting life.

It becomes important to observe the historical patterns of God's relationship with the nation of Israel in order to draw valid conclusions for our lives today.

Foreign gods had no power over Israel, but the Israelites became vulnerable because they did not adhere to the instructions of Almighty God. They did not adhere to the words of the prophets that were sent to them by God. Their hearts became hardened, and they became the enemy of God. Isaiah 63:10 says, "But they rebelled, and vexed his holy Spirit: therefore he was turned to be their enemy, and he fought against them."

Direct cause and effect is evident in rebellion. When a nation is in idolatrous rebellion against God, His unchangeable nature is violated and that nation becomes an enemy of God.

It is interesting to note that in verse ten, it says that "he was turned." In other words, the effect of being at war with God was not initiated by God, nor was it God's desire to be at odds with mankind. Rather, it is a direct result of the rebellious actions of man.

The history of the nation of Israel also illustrates the pathway to peace with God. When the people of Israel repented (renewing their relationship with God, worshipping Him alone), God forgave them and restored their nation.

Godly sorrow is the beginning of the process of repentance and restoration. It is the type of sorrow that responds to the recognition that sin has entered in, and that sin grieves the heart of Almighty God.

God is making the church of America more aware of its condition because He loves His people. The Holy Spirit is correcting us so that we can be vessels of the power of Almighty God, the power that will express the glory and goodness of God.

Agape Love

Our strength is found in walking in willing obedience to God and His Word. It is a love walk to such a degree that others will know that we belong to Him. It is manifested in our love for God with every part of our being, and loving others as God does. It is *agape* love working in and through us.

Many years ago, the Lord ministered to me about *agape* love in a situation that confronted me. I was concerned about a young couple who were making a decision that I knew would not be good for their home or marriage. I was debating whether or not to speak to them about the situation.

The woman had a brother who was saved and Spirit-filled, but who was in a backslidden condition. He was supporting a drug habit by stealing, was caught and sent to prison. It was unusual in that he was imprisoned on a first offense charge, which was a test case for the judicial system in his state.

While in his cell, he was visited by Jesus and recommitted his life to God. However, when he was released, he did not have a church to help him maintain his victory. He returned to his old crowd of drug users.

Since he was on probation, his life was under scrutiny. He was picked up by the police for a possible parole violation. This meant that if he were found guilty, he would have to return to prison without the possibility of parole. Prayer for God's mercy went forth on his behalf.

When his case came up before the judge, the arresting police officers did not show up to give their testimony. The case was dismissed for lack of evidence. As the young man was leaving the court building, he walked through the main entrance. The police officers who were supposed to give testimony were entering the building at the same time saying that they had never before been caught in such a traffic jam.

God was indeed merciful to him and he was given another chance, however, he still was not living right. His sister and her husband thought that it would be helpful to bring him to their home. I knew that their marriage was not strong enough, nor were they wise enough to deal with the situation of a troubled brother in their home.

The conflict that I had to deal with was offering unsolicited advice, with the risk of sounding like I was interfering. Yet I knew that their marriage and peace was at stake if I did not speak to them.

As I sought the Lord, He said to me, "Now, suppose they were walking down a path in the woods, and you were with them. If you saw a snake coiled up ready to strike them, would you stand aside and allow them to walk into that danger, or would you do everything in your power to keep them from peril?"

I didn't have to ponder over the answer. It was obvious that I would want to protect them. The Lord then said, "Likewise, go and warn them."

There sometimes is a fine line between being helpful and being a pest. When the compassion of God is working along with the leading of the Holy Spirit, His Word will bring life to a situation. He will prompt someone to say the right words at just the right time, and it will bring healing and safety.

It is out of the same compassion, leading, and expression of agape love, that warnings are being given to the church to make the necessary adjustments to prepare us for revival.

Prophecy is one of the ways God speaks to His people. His Words through a prophet bring life, healing, and safety.

The Devil's Counterfeit

The devil has counterfeits that try to imitate the gifts and power of Almighty God. Prophecy is a gift of God that He manifests when He wants to say something to His people. The spirit of divination also has a strong foretelling and false prophesying component. It is a counterfeit of God's gift.

With false prophecy comes disappointment and disillusionment to the point where people begin to despise prophecy. Because of the hurt caused by false prophecy, there arises criticism and the forbidding of all prophecy, even that which is truly from God. It is an operation of the spirit of python to cut off a gift to the body of Christ.

It is like a currency counterfeiter. If someone counterfeited twenty dollar bills and flooded the market place with them, there would be victims who would suffer loss because of the valueless money. However, it would also make the consumer more astute to spot a counterfeit for the sake of obtaining the real thing. We don't throw away all twenty dollar bills because there are some counterfeit ones floating around.

Likewise, we know that there are victims whenever false prophecy is given. We have been given the equipment necessary to distinguish the false from the real, and therefore, should not forbid all prophesying because there is a counterfeit. We simply need to become more spiritually fine tuned by learning God's Word and listening to the Holy Spirit.

Whispering

ISAIAH 29:4

4 And thou shalt be brought down, and shalt speak out of the ground, and thy speech shall be low out of the dust, and thy voice shall be, as of one that hath a familiar spirit, out of the ground, and thy speech shall whisper out of the dust.

The word "familiar" is the Hebrew word *ov*, which usually refers to the spirit of a dead person that mediums supposedly are able to summon. Low voiced whispered incantations were commonplace among those who practiced witchcraft, especially in ancient mystery religions. Rhythmic chanting in whispered and low earthy tones is still practiced by many Eastern religions.

Whispering gossip and flattering words are obvious examples of wrongdoing. However, some people will want to whisper a "Word of the Lord" to you. It may well be a word of a lord, but not the Lord Jesus Christ. Spirits of divination want things to be hushed, mysterious, calling attention to the vessel instead of the glory of God. It is so important to know the voice of the Holy Spirit and the Word of God to verify what you hear.

I might add a word of caution here about subliminal messages. On the surface, all that is heard is something non-threatening like ocean sounds, or sweet music, but on a subconscious level, messages are bombarding your mind.

Advertisers promise weight loss, personal success, breaking unhealthy habits, and a wide variety of other intriguing self-help selections. Since you do not have access on a conscious level to what is being spoken on a subconscious level, you have no idea what is being fed to your mind. It is a risky thing to blindly submit your mind to such controlling mechanisms.

God's word solemnly warns us to measure everything you hear up against the Word of God. We are obligated to judge all teaching by the standard of the revealed Word of God.

ISAIAH 8:19,20 (Amplified Bible)

19 And when the people [instead of putting their trust in God] shall say to you, Consult for direction mediums and wizards who chirp and mutter, should not a people seek and consult their God? Should they consult the dead on behalf of the living?

20 [Direct such people] to the teaching and to the testimony; if their teachings are not in accord with this word, it is surely because there is no dawn and no morning for them.

Those who do not speak in agreement with the revealed Word of God are in darkness. It is not a matter of personal interpretation. God's Word is the standard to which everything must agree.

Foretelling

Isaiah 8:19,20 is dealing with the same kind of person that is presented in Acts 16:16, that is, one who is a foreteller of future events. Familiar spirits, the spirit of python, spirits of divination, and religious spirits are actively deceiving people in the arena of foretelling.

People have a natural curiosity and desire to know about things to come. When you compound that with a pretense of power over the future, and the lack of knowledge and wisdom of Almighty God, you have a ready audience for demonic control.

What is God's way regarding knowledge of the future? Psalm 25:4 says, "Shew me thy ways, O Lord; teach me thy paths." If you need direction, go to the Lord and allow Him to show you the course of events for your life. His Word is reliable and produces success.

Psalm 27:11 says, "Teach me thy way, O Lord, and lead me in a plain path, because of mine enemies." The Holy Spirit's ministry to believers is to teach and guide into truth. He is more than able to direct the way we are to conduct our lives, and to reveal information to us supernaturally.

There is a valid ministry of prophets. God's Word bears that out repeatedly. However, we must be aware that while there are true prophets of God, there are also false ones under the influence of ungodly spirits. These false prophets are intent on deception and crushing the life out of anyone with whom they come in contact.

A strategy of the spirit of divination, spirit of python, and religious spirit, is to overwhelm an individual. In the same way that fans are overwhelmed by their idol (be it an actor, musician, or sports hero), people are sometimes awestruck by ministers. They are so influenced that they remain staunchly loyal based on fear of breaking away, rather than for the right reasons.

Wisdom to Prevail

The Word of God gives us wisdom to prevail. Proverbs 11:1 tells us, "A false balance is abomination to the Lord: but a just weight is his delight." Although balance has to do with weights and measures in dealing with honesty, it also has to do with keeping ourselves in balance with the Word and the Spirit.

Proverbs 21:23 says, "Whoso keepeth his mouth and his tongue keepeth his soul from troubles." Self control over what we say is absolutely vital to a successful walk in life. We need to speak in agreement with the Word of God in all areas of our lives.

In Proverbs 25:28, it says, "He that hath no rule over his own spirit is like a city that is broken down, and without walls." It will leave you defenseless if you do not have charge over your own spirit. Others may want to rule your spirit, control your life in the spirit, and keep you from experiencing God fully. God made you a free-will being, you have choices, and He encourages you to choose life.

Wisdom for prevailing must also deal with flattery. Because of our natural desire to please man, the snare of flattery can be subtle. We need to be on guard so that pleasing God is absolutely paramount. Proverbs 26:28 says, "A lying tongue hateth those that are afflicted by it; and a flattering mouth worketh ruin."

It is so easy to accept flattery and become puffed up in pride, thinking that you are the one making your life a success, even in the ministry. Pulpit ministers are often targets for the flattery of people, and need to keep words that people speak to them in God's perspective.

JOB 32:21,22

21 Let me not, I pray you, accept any man's person, neither let me give flattering titles unto man.

22 For I know not to give flattering titles; in so doing my maker would soon take me away.

A title attached to an immature person can be devastating. Man has attached prestige and power to titles and it has the potential of corrupting those who allow it to deceive them. Even titles like apostle, evangelist, pastor, prophet, and teacher, have been made to hold rank in churches. The reality is, however, that these are responsible offices that identify how the person is to function, not just a title.

Other scripture verses that will help you to prevail against the powers of darkness are as follows.

PROVERBS 27:12

12 A prudent man foreseeth the evil, and hideth himself; but the simple pass on, and are punished.

PROVERBS 28:13

13 He that covereth his sins shall not prosper: but whoso confesseth and forsaketh them shall have mercy.

The importance of Proverbs 28:13 needs to be underscored with vigor. When you sin, don't just cover it up. Run to God, confess it, and get it under the blood of Jesus Christ. Go to the fountain of the blood of Jesus, letting that godly sorrow work repentance in you.

The Word of God has more wisdom than any one person can write about, but here are some more powerful words to prevail in the battle.

PROVERBS 11:27

27 He that diligently seeketh good procureth favour: but he that seeketh mischief, it shall come unto him.

PROVERBS 10:6

6 Blessings are upon the head of the just: but violence covereth the mouth of the wicked.

PROVERBS 12:21

21 There shall no evil happen to the just: but the wicked shall be filled with mischief.

ROMANS 16:20

20 And the God of peace shall bruise Satan under your feet shortly. The grace of our Lord Jesus Christ be with you. Amen.

PROVERBS 13:13

13 Whoso despiseth the word shall be destroyed: but he that feareth the commandment shall be rewarded.

It can simply be summed up with the admonition to fall in love with the Word of God. If His Word does not have a prominent place in your life, you must make the decision to spend a balance of time in prayer, praise and worship, and study and meditation of the Word of God. It is a winning combination that will cause you to prevail in every situation.

Chapter 10
The Foundation That Delivers

In spite of all of the hardships, stress, and negative publicity that the body of Christ has endured in the last decade, God is putting new strength and stability into those who are hearing from the Spirit of God. He is encouraging us to be balanced with regard to experiences in the spirit realm and knowledge of the Word of God. He is bringing us to a new awareness of our foundation.

Foundation in Liberty

The foundation of all that we are, and all that we believe, is the Lord Jesus Christ. In Him, we have liberty and are no longer enslaved by any yoke of bondage.

GALATIANS 5:1 (Amplified Bible)

1 In [this] freedom Christ has made us free — completely liberated us; stand fast then, and do not be hampered and held ensnared and submit again to a yoke of slavery — which you have once put off.

Sin and darkness no longer have dominion over us, and the liberty that Jesus has given us is complete, lacking nothing. Jesus proclaimed the purpose for His coming when He read from the book of Isaiah in the synagogue of Nazareth.

LUKE 4:18,19

18 The Spirit of the Lord is upon me, because He hath anointed me to preach the gospel to the poor; He hath sent

me to heal the brokenhearted, to preach deliverance to the captives, and recovering of sight to the blind, to set at liberty them that are bruised,

19 To preach the acceptable year of the Lord.

The religious people of Nazareth were so agitated by this claim of Jesus that they wanted to annihilate Him. They could not accept the liberty He offered. Religious people today still have the same problem in accepting the liberty of Jesus.

Jesus had the *exousia*, that is, the power, authority, capacity, competence, and jurisdiction, when He spoke those words to the Nazarene people. Since He is the same yesterday, today, and forever according to Hebrews 13:8, the same *exousia* is still working today. We have access to that power because He gave us the right to use His Name and all of the power and authority that goes with it.

This should encourage and strengthen us. Regardless of the cult, idol, or doctrine that is the current fad, if the foundation is not on the solid rock, the Lord Jesus Christ, it has to crumble. Any other foundation besides that of Jesus, is one of bondage and powerless ritual.

Freedom Under Grace, Not Law

In the early church, some of the Jewish believers wanted to impose the Old Testament law of circumcision on new Gentile believers. They believed that the Gentiles needed to first convert to Judaism, and then become Christians.

Paul, a former Pharisee, had great insight into the law and its inadequacy for salvation. He was anointed by the Holy Spirit to point out the error of this kind of religious thinking.

GALATIANS 5:2-6

2 Behold, I Paul say unto you, that if ye be circumcised, Christ shall profit you nothing.

3 For I testify again to every man that is circumcised, that he is a debtor to do the whole law.

4 Christ is become of no effect unto you, whosoever of you are justified by the law; ye are fallen from grace.

5 For we through the Spirit wait for the hope of righteousness by faith.

6 For in Jesus Christ neither circumcision availeth any thing, nor uncircumcision; but faith which worketh by love.

Under the anointing of the Holy Spirit, Paul explained that going back to the law is not only unnecessary, but it is undesirable. Our foundation in Jesus Christ is one of liberty from ritual and emancipation from all bondage.

Works have never been a satisfactory means to righteousness. In fact, works serve to show our own inadequacies and the need for saving grace. When people try to become justified by works of the law, they fall from grace.

Grace is more than unmerited favor. It is the help, ability, power, strength, efficiency, and sufficiency of God operating on our behalf, in spite of the fact that we do not deserve it. In short, it is the Holy Spirit at work. When a person tries to attain righteousness by his own works, he does not allow the power of the Holy Spirit, the Spirit of grace, to function. Religions contend that the favor and righteousness of God is attained by the accumulation of man's efforts to perform rituals and deeds perceived as being good. In God's plan, however, we are made new creations by faith in Christ Jesus. We have the nature of Almighty God dwelling within our spirit man, and we perform good works motivated by His love and grace.

Righteousness and grace are gifts that cannot be earned by any natural means. All that we possess and perform which has eternal value is accomplished by the ability of God working in and through us. It is by grace that we are saved, and it is by grace that we are sustained.

This grace is received by faith. Any working of flesh is not of faith, and it does not please God. Romans 8:8 says, "So then they that are in the flesh cannot please God." This is further confirmed by Hebrews 11:6, "But without faith, it is impossible to please him (God)...."

The Word of God further tells us that living our lives to pursue the flesh holds only death as its reward. Romans 8:13 declares, "For if ye live after the flesh, ye shall die: but if ye through the Spirit do mortify the deeds of the body, ye shall live." The choice of living after the flesh or living through the Spirit is ours.

When something is mortified, it is as dead as cement and has no power to work. How do we mortify the deeds of the flesh? It is through the power of the Holy Spirit working through a yielded vessel totally submitted to the obedience of God's Word and Will.

A Prepared Vessel

Mortifying the deeds of the flesh and allowing the Holy Spirit to function in our lives begins with the choice to do so, but it does not end there.

We may want to storm the gates of hell and prevail, but where do we begin? Having the desire is important, but desire alone doesn't even put a dent into the gates of hell. A prepared vessel, open to the move of the Holy Spirit, understands that obedience to God and His Word is the key to victory over the attacks of the enemy.

JAMES 4:7

7 Submit yourselves therefore to God. Resist the devil, and he will flee from you.

I PETER 5:6-9

6 Humble yourselves therefore under the mighty hand of God, that he may exalt you in due time:

7 Casting all your care upon him; for he careth for you.

8 Be sober, be vigilant; because your adversary the devil, as a roaring lion, walketh about, seeking whom he may devour:

9 Whom resist stedfast in the faith, knowing that the same afflictions are accomplished in your brethren that are in the world.

Humbling yourself does not mean only laying down prostrate in prayer. It simply means to obey God. The humble heart is one that is teachable, pliable, open to receiving instruction, and ready to submit its own will without reservations. It is the kind of heart that God is able to use. Resisting the devil is something that we can accomplish. If it were not so, God would not have directed us to do it. We have access to the strength and ability of the Holy Spirit to resist the enemy in all situations.

The word "resist" is *antitasso* in Greek. It is a composite of *anti*, meaning "against," and *tasso*, meaning "to set oneself against something in a militant sense." We are directed to resist the devil militantly, with an uncompromising fervor.

In 2 Timothy 2:3, we are called soldiers of Jesus Christ. It says, "Thou therefore endure hardness, as a good soldier of Jesus Christ." We are clearly in a war. The enemy has not only been exposed, but he can only triumph over believers when we act in ignorance or unbelief.

The church has not been called to a passive life. We must do more than contemplate the wonders of the heavens. We are a militant people, set in battle against the devil's army. God is divinely setting us in order to function as an effective army led by the Captain of our salvation, Jesus Christ.

Called Unto Liberty

The fifth chapter of Galatians provides a clear picture of the liberty to which we, as disciples of the Lord Jesus, are called. It is a liberty full of the benefits and privileges of salvation.

GALATIANS 5:7-10

7 Ye did run well; who did hinder you that ye should not obey the truth?

8 This persuasion cometh not of him that calleth you.

9 A little leaven leaveneth the whole lump.

10 I have confidence in you through the Lord, that ye will be none otherwise minded: but he that troubleth you shall bear his judgment, whosoever he be.

Paul was addressing the issue of church leaders reintroducing religious ritual and the bondage associated with it. Because it is not of faith, as Romans 14:23b declares, it is sin.

Sin, symbolized by leaven, is a pervasive thing. It spoils all that it touches. When believers are under the bondage from which they were previously freed by the blood of Jesus Christ, they no longer believe truth. They become disabled in their faith. Paul also makes a clear statement that there is judgment awaiting those who draw believers away from the truth.

GALATIANS 5:11-13

11 And I, brethren, if I yet preach circumcision, why do I yet suffer persecution? then is the offence of the cross ceased.

12 I would they were even cut off which trouble you.

13 For, brethren, ye have been called unto liberty; only use not liberty for an occasion to the flesh, but by love serve one another.

Paul suffered persecution continually for the sake of the gospel during the course of his ministry. If he had compromised and gone along with those who were promoting religious bondage, the persecution would have ceased. Yet Paul was convinced of the liberty of the cross. He understood that there is only one law, the law of love.

GALATIANS 5: 14,15

14 For all the law is fulfilled in one word, even in this; Thou shalt love thy neighbor as thyself.

15 But if ye bite and devour one another, take heed that ye be not consumed one of another.

God is calling us to be a holy people. Because Jesus is the Light, His glory will shine and any darkness will be exposed. This includes wounds that have been inflicted by the words of others.

Backbiting is not just harmless chatter. The word "backbite" in the original Greek means "to tear or rend with reproach," and also "to tell lies about each other." When someone assassinates your character, it wounds your soul and causes suffering.

Other meanings of "backbite" in Greek are "to point a finger at someone, and to put a hex or curse on someone with the intent to do them harm." Speaking evil of someone is tantamount to cursing them. It is operating in witchcraft, that is, manipulating a person to do what *you* want them to do instead of what God's will and their own will dictates.

GALATIANS 3:1

1 O foolish Galatians, who hath bewitched you, that ye should not obey the truth, before whose eyes Jesus Christ hath been evidently set forth, crucified among you?

Engaging in backbiting is simply not smart, for what we sow, we do reap.

When people backbite and spread evil about each other, it is a devouring maneuver. The word "devour" means total annihilation. In backbiting, the victim is hurt by having his emotions consumed. When the emotions are consumed, physical power is also drained.

The devil knows that everything from the spirit flows through the soul realm, which is why he inspires people to backbite. It produces rebellion against all forms of authority. Out of his arsenal of evil, he sends divisive spirits to crush souls and eventually wear down the physical body until everything is depleted.

Wearing down the saints is one of the adversary's main strategies. Daniel 7:25a states, "And he shall speak great words against the most High, and shall wear out the saints of the most High...." One of the major tactics used by the father of lies to accomplish this is to accuse the brethren. (See Revelation 12:9-12.)

When the soul is wounded, the body is weary and drained. It is a spirit of heaviness. The remedy for it is to put on the garment of praise. It exalts and magnifies Almighty God.

ISAIAH 61:3

3 To appoint unto them that mourn in Zion, to give unto them beauty for ashes, the oil of joy for mourning, the garment of praise for the spirit of heaviness; that they might be called trees of righteousness, the planting of the Lord, that he might be glorified.

Devour also means "to exploit," and "to consume by eating." When people backbite, they are "eating people alive" with their words. It is a process where first they take a bite. Then they devour their prey until the victim is completely consumed.

The devil wants to remove any and all possibility of your effectiveness in the work of the Lord. When these times of testing come, what your flesh wants to do is take a trip to Tahiti, where no one knows you and you can forget about it altogether. It's times like these that people want to isolate themselves.

This is the time to plant yourself firmly and fight through to victory. It is imperative that you continue to fellowship with the saints, and purpose in your mind that you are not going to faint or disappear.

Another nuance of meaning for "consume" is "to destroy by fire," and to "fry alive." The devil throws fiery darts at you with the intent of destroying you by frying you alive. He wants your energy spent and so he turns on the heat of his attacks. The devil's fire consumes with destruction to the extent that nothing salvageable remains.

The Bible says, "For the Lord thy God is a consuming fire..." (Deuteronomy 4:24a), Who burns up wickedness and purifies us like refined gold. When it is the heat of the All-Consuming Fire, Almighty God, there is no destruction or loss. What remains is pure and holy.

Works of the Flesh

GALATIANS 5:16-21

16 This I say then, Walk in the Spirit, and ye shall not fulfill the lust of the flesh.

17 For the flesh lusteth against the Spirit, and the Spirit against the flesh: and these are contrary the one to the other: so that ye cannot do the things that ye would.

18 But if ye be led of the Spirit, ye are not under the law.

19 Now the works of the flesh are manifest, which are these; Adultery, fornication, uncleanness, lasciviousness,

20 Idolatry, witchcraft, hatred, variance, emulations, wrath, strife, seditions, heresies,

21 Envyings, murders, drunkenness, revellings, and such like: of the which I tell you before, as I have also told you in time past, that they which do such things shall not inherit the kingdom of God.

Notice that actions mentioned in verses 19 to 21 are called works of the *flesh,* not works of demon possession. They are, however, demon inspired. They are in direct opposition to the leading of the Holy Spirit. As we follow the Holy Spirit, we will not fulfill the lust of the flesh that manifests itself in these behaviors.

Witchcraft

The word "witchcraft" in Greek is *pharmakeia,* from which we derive the word "pharmacy." It primarily signifies the use of medicine, drugs, spells, and sorcery.

A person yielding to the influence of witchcraft is operating under a false delusion. Their primary awareness centers on evil or that which is not good. They see demons, wickedness, and weakness in people and circumstances. They are compulsively focused on the negative.

Even their perception of God is distorted. They see God as One Who is fierce and full of wrath, seeking to destroy people. However, the fact is that God is good and full of mercy and compassion, Who loved the world so much that He gave His precious Son to save sinners (John 3:16).

When sorcery is performed, it is usually accompanied by incantations, and the application of amulets and charms. The idea is to use spells and amulets to keep the evil spirits away.

Crystals are the most recent rage in amulets. They are being sold all across this nation as objects having mystical power. It is a counterfeit, a sad and ridiculous imitation of God's crystal.

EZEKIEL 1:22

22 And the likeness of the firmament upon the heads of the living creature was as the colour of the terrible crystal, stretched forth over their heads above.

REVELATION 4:6

6 And before the throne there was a sea of glass like unto crystal: and in the midst of the throne, and round about the throne, were four beasts full of eyes before and behind.

The terrible crystal is none other than the presence of God. It is difficult to imagine that people actually ascribe power to a polished piece of glass, when we can *know the Creator* of the substance from which the glass was made.

Wearing objects associated with superstition and witchcraft identifies the wearer as one who puts confidence in such things. When I pray for people who are wearing such objects, I am sometimes led by the Spirit to direct the wearer of the objects to remove them and to never wear them again. If a person truly desires to be free, he must also be willing to forsake all of the idolatrous symbols that are associated with ungodly superstition and occultish practices.

By receiving the potions and amulets, the recipient makes himself dependent on the power and resources of the sorcerer. Likewise in church circles, we must not put our priority trust in human beings. We certainly should respect each other, the ministry gifts, and those placed in authority over us, but always bear in mind that it is the power and anointing of the Holy Spirit that is working through the minister of righteousness.

When flesh and blood is exalted and glorified instead of God, you can be assured that demons are at work. Like the apostle Paul declared, we are who and what we are by the grace of God.

JAMES 1:17

17 Every good gift and every perfect gift is from above, and cometh down from the Father of lights, with whom is no variableness, neither shadow of turning.

God is the source of all blessings that are ministered under His anointing. It is for this reason that we are forbidden to glory in flesh.

Those who try to minister with deception, trying to counterfeit the anointing and manifestation of the gifts of the Holy Spirit, do so in the flesh. The only reason they are received is because people look to the personality of the minister instead of the personality of the Holy Spirit. We must reserve the glory for God alone.

Familiar Spirits

People sometimes operate in witchcraft unknowingly. I once ministered to a person who spoke to me about the fact that she and her husband were searching for the perfect church to attend. She spoke at length about how whenever they went to a church, they were able to keenly discern what was wrong with it.

First of all, you will never find a perfect church here on earth. The pastor is imperfect, along with the members. They all have to seek the Lord and grow in grace together. The only perfect church is in heaven.

Furthermore, the great discernment that this couple supposedly possessed, functioned continuously in them, and seemed to only pick up weaknesses. There is a distinct difference between the gift of discerning of spirits and the ability to perceive the difference between good and evil.

The gift of discerning of spirits operates as the Spirit wills, not as the human being wills. It allows you to see into the spirit realm, both good and evil, when the Holy Spirit has a specific purpose for it to operate.

Hebrews 5:12-14 tells us that we exercise our senses to know the difference between good and evil. This kind of discernment comes by spending time in prayer, in studying the Bible, and in obedience to the Word of God as a lifestyle. It is perception based on knowledge, understanding, and experience in God's Word, with wisdom to apply it to your life.

When someone is continuously discerning only that which is evil, they are being influenced by familiar spirits, who seek to point out weaknesses for condemnation. Familiar spirits do not want you to see the goodness of God, or the goodness of other people and things.

We should take the position of looking for the good in everyone. When the gift of discerning of spirits operates and reveals oppression, the purpose is to set the person free by the anointing of God.

Fruit of the Spirit

How do you overcome the works of the flesh? In contrast to the works of the flesh, Galatians 5:22-26 describes the manifested behavior of one who walks in the Spirit. Particularly noteworthy is that the former is identified as *works* of the flesh, and the latter a *walk* in the Spirit. The works of the flesh speak of a series of isolated deeds strung together in a person's life, whereas the walk in the Spirit speaks of a lifestyle of devoted service to God and the results of doing so.

GALATIANS 5:22-26

22 But the fruit of the Spirit is love, joy, peace, longsuffering, gentleness, goodness, faith,

23 Meekness, temperance: against such there is no law.

24 And they that are Christ's have crucified the flesh with the affections and lusts.

25 If we live in the Spirit, let us also walk in the Spirit.

26 Let us not be desirous of vain glory, provoking one another, envying one another.

Many commentaries on the fruit of the Spirit focus particularly on love. If you have the *agape* love of God, the other eight fruit will be evident as well.

How does it change a situation from death to life? If someone does something wrong to you, allow the power of love and forgiveness to prevent bitterness from taking hold. In Matthew 5:44, Jesus gave very clear direction about this matter.

MATTHEW 5:44

44 But I say unto you, Love your enemies, bless them that curse you, do good to them that hate you, and pray for them which despitefully use you, and persecute you;

In so doing, you are choosing to live in the Spirit. "...Mercy triumphs over judgment" (James 2:13b, *NIV*). As we forgive and pray for those who persecute us, and say all manner of evil against us, "...the love of God is shed abroad in our hearts by the Holy Ghost which is given unto us" (Romans 5:5b).

God will cause this act of mercy working through us to triumph over the words of death spoken against us. According to Ephesians 1:6b, we have been "...accepted in the beloved."

Can we be justified in rejecting His beloved? Conversely, as one who has been accepted by the Lord Jesus Christ, should the rejection from others really matter? The answer to both of these questions is a resounding "No!"

1 CORINTHIANS 4:1-5

1 Let a man so account of us, as of the ministers of Christ, and stewards of the mysteries of God.

2 Moreover it is required in stewards, that a man be found faithful.

3 But with me it is a very small thing that I should be judged of you, or of man's judgment: yea, I judge not mine own self.

4 For I know nothing by myself; yet am I not hereby justified: but he that judgeth me is the Lord.

5 Therefore judge nothing before the time, until the Lord come, who both will bring to light the hidden things of darkness, and will make manifest the counsels of the hearts: and then shall every man have praise of God.

When anger tries to enter, turn to the force of patience. This is not mind over matter. It is turning away from the works of flesh, and choosing to walk in the fruit of the Spirit.

In examining the nine fruit of the Spirit, we find that they fall into three categories. First is love, joy, and peace, which are an outgrowth of our communion and fellowship with God. The second category is faith, temperance, and meekness, which are the fruit we need in resolving conflicts. The third category includes long-suffering, gentleness, and goodness, which deal with our relationships with others. These three categories are the fruit of obedience to the two commandments that Jesus gave. Love God with your whole being, and love your neighbor as yourself.

My prayer for you is as follows:

Father, thank you for the precious Holy Spirit, for Your Word, and the strength that it brings. I rejoice in knowing the sure foundation is the Lord Jesus Christ, and look to Him with the expectation that You will complete that which You have begun in us.

Father, thank you for the precious people that have received Your Word, for it will produce life in them. I ask that they become strong in Jesus Christ, overcome by His precious blood, and that Your Word produce everlasting fruit in their lives, in Jesus' Name. Amen.

Epilogue

The Church of the Lord Jesus Christ is experiencing the glory of God for the ultimate harvest. Although our number one priority is the harvest of souls, we are to reap the harvest of all we have sown in obedience to the Word of God. As we reap, we will increase in our capability to sow. As we sow into the kingdom of God, more souls will be saved.

Our adversary is fighting against this ultimate harvest. As we are experiencing increasing measures of God's glory, the adversary is counterattacking. In every attack, as we turn to God, we overcome with greater strength. We become stronger and wiser by His grace. We are being forged into a strength (as we are in Him) that will be impenetrable. As we fight together, we will come out stronger in unity and stronger in ourselves.

The enemy especially attacks the strategies we have to fulfill the work of the ministry and God's will for our lives. When he fails at that, he attacks the logistics: that which we need to get the job done; the resources, aid, and assistance.

Recently, a pastor asked that I meet with him and his wife along with the church leaders, worship team, intercessors, and their wives, for prayer and understanding concerning the reoccurring battle within the church.

As we worshipped, and then prayed, the Holy Spirit began to speak to me. I wrote these things down and then was asked to share them. They seemed to be related to this book. Therefore, I share some of them, trusting they will help you.

You are not isolated in the battle. Others who are experiencing the glory are likewise experiencing the battle. It is a good fight of faith.

Our answer to the enemy, after we have done what we know to do to overcome, is, "Satan, when Jesus heard about the death of John the Baptist, He turned. He went forth to feed the multitudes, preach, teach, heal the sick and the oppressed, and to work miracles. You just wait until tonight (or tomorrow). You are going to see God move in His glory as you have never seen through us (me), or in this place." Then go forth and do it!

When God moves, the enemy moves either out of the way, or in a counterattack, or both. Part of the package of the glory is the counterattack of the enemy. We tend to forget this.

"If you are censured and suffer abuse [because you bear] the name of Christ, blessed [are you] — happy, fortunate, to be envied, with life-joy, and satisfaction in God's favor and salvation, regardless of your outward condition — because the Spirit of glory, the Spirit of God, is resting upon you..." (1 Peter 4:14 *The Amplified Bible*).

Count it all joy (James 1:2) when you fall into divers temptations, tests, and trials! Remember, Paul said a great and effectual door had been opened unto him, and there were many adversaries. The harder your battle, the greater your work, and the greater the effectual door that is opened unto you.

Determine to see the attack through to its end together. Do not allow the enemy to divide and conquer.

Work it out together. Do it together. When the enemy sees that determination, he panics.

The raging battles of python and his friends are especially noted in Revelation 2:18-29, under the name "Jezebel." Jezebel is a spirit of abortion. This spirit tries to take control of people to abort God's plan, and to keep people from receiving. In this portion of scripture, we see the positives and negatives. But as we do, we can also comprehend our counterattack.

WORKS: The adversaries come against your good works. Our counterattack: *WORK!*

CHARITY: The adversaries try to stop your love and the deeds of that love. Our counterattack: Love in thought, work, and action. *KEEP LOVING AND DOING THE GOOD WORKS!*

SERVICE: How has Satan attacked you? If you think seriously, he has come against you in the area of service which God has called you to. He doesn't care what tactic, lie, deception, or person he uses. He simply wants to stop you. Our counterattack: *KEEP ON SERVING!* You never make a decision to move away when the pressure is on. You make such a decision when everything is so wonderful you don't want to move.

This question needs to be asked when we feel that there should be a change, or I should change, or I should get out, or I should not do this or that: When did you feel that? When did you feel that need to change? Did it come in the middle of the problem? That's not it. Did it come when the pressure was on? That's not God. Anyone can run away. We're to run to the battle, not away from it.

FAITH: Satan will create doubts, such as, "Has God said? Is this really God's will for my life? How do I know? Maybe all this pressure is God telling me I'm not in His will. Maybe He wants me to leave and...?" Counterattack: *STAND FIRM*. Having done all to stand, we are going to stand in faith. We refuse every false word of faith, for it takes away our hope in God!

PATIENCE: What are you going to do when your patience is tested? *COUNT IT ALL JOY*, and throw a Holy Ghost count-it-all-joy party, a praise and worship party, a prayer party, a fellowship party! With such a party, the anointing shall reveal and destroy every yoke of bondage!

CALLETH HERSELF A PROPHETESS: You will be attacked in the area of prophetic anointing. Whatever God has spoken and shown to you will be attacked. Counterattack: *DO NOT DESPISE PROPHESYINGS*, and *WAGE A GOOD WARFARE* with the very prophecies God has given to you.

TEACHING AND SOUND DOCTRINE: Satan wants to stop revelation teaching. With this attack, he wants to bring in the unclean and the mixed: seduce to fornication. Counterattack: *RECEIVE AND WALK IN THE PURE WORD* and will of God, and *TEACH*.

DEPTHS: The depths of our own heart (reins and hearts). No one can search or know our heart for us. As leaders (or believers), there is a time when we can be regimented by certain laws and principles that we must do under the oversight of the authority over us. The authority knows it is for our good, and carefully administrates our doing of them.

However, there must be a point of maturity where we observe these guidelines without another forcing it upon us. We observe them out of love for God and because it is in our heart to do it. If you are a leader, you are a leader. You have to accept responsibilities.

Counterattack: *KNOW* the height, depth, breadth, and width of *GOD'S LOVE* for you, that you may also share His great love with others.

NONE OTHER BURDEN: The enemy continuously attempts to weigh us down with burdens. Counterattack: Take every burden to the Lord in prayer. *PUT OFF THE WEIGHTS.* Rejoice.

THAT WHICH YOU ALREADY HAVE: A battle rages to take from you that which you already have, already know, and are already doing. *HOLD FAST* to that which you already have.

OVERCOME: There is something to overcome. Remember, when Satan tempted Jesus (Luke 4:1-14), He didn't ask, "Where did I open the door?" He said, "It is written, *GET THEE BEHIND ME, SATAN.*" If you live conscious of 1 John 1:9, and a battle rages, if God doesn't reveal to you "where" you've missed it, or "how" the door is opened, then follow the example of Jesus.

POWER AND RULE: The enemy attempts to weaken our power and rule in the authority of Jesus Christ. Remember, in Him *BATTLES AND VICTORIES* increase our power and rule.

TOGETHER, AUTHORITY, COMMUNICATION: These three are necessary if we are going to remain together to accomplish God's work. Fear, estrangement, and lack of communication create strangeness. You are dubious about trusting those around you. Communication and fellowship become difficult.

We must talk things out, regardless of the fear of wounds and hurts. "Come, let us reason together." And we must be mature enough for such CONFRONTATIONS. The enemy hates openness and light. He works in darkness and hidden things.

Learn to whom it should be communicated (divine order of authority prevents sowing seeds of strife among the brethren). Learn when not to communicate. Sometimes it's not the person that you are against who has a problem at all; but rather, you have a problem, and that's why you are against the person. Overcome your own works of flesh. Don't yield to the Absalom or Korah spirit. Don't sow seeds of discontent or suspicion. Don't be in bondage to liberty.

SETTLE WHAT YOU ARE: What are you? If you know what you are, and it is settled between you and God, then the devil is not going to have such an opportunity to get you out of there. I am what I am by the grace of God. Settle what you are. Then, when Satan tries to tempt you to covet another position, another title, or another work, you can say, "NO, this is what I am. This is where I am to be." Settle what you are.

GUARD AGAINST BATTLE FATIGUE: Warring, warring, warring; thinking, thinking, thinking about the enemy; talking, talking, talking about the enemy until battle fatigue sets in. Emphasis should be the greatness, the majesty, the joy, the wonder, the excitement, the enthusiasm of Almighty God.

EMPHASIS ON HOLINESS: Holiness and wholeness are one and the same. The enemy knows he has lost his royal battle when we reach *WHOLENESS* in spirit, soul, and body, as well as a lifestyle of one set apart unto God.

GO FORWARD. The devil doesn't want you to go forward. He wants you to make an idol out of your past mistakes, failures, hurts, and wounds. How do you know when you have? You think and talk about them constantly. Forget these things! Then he can't say, "Well, it happened before, and now again. Therefore, there's no hope, because it will keep on happening." No! It is finished. Today is a new day and a new battle.

PRAY FOR ONE ANOTHER: The New Testament strongly teaches this. People do not know what is against them; therefore, they come and go. Pray for one another.

POWER OF THE SECRET PLACE: It begins and ends when no one knows, sees, or hears what we are thinking, saying, or doing. Make God our secret place!

ABOVE ALL THINGS: Keep your joy, your enthusiasm, and your child-like excitement about the Lord your God!

Audio cassette albums to accompany this book are available.

The Spirit of Python
(four tapes)

Sequel to Python
(six tapes)

Other Books by Bobbie Jean Merck

Power of the Secret Place

Hope

Mini-Books:

The Miracle of Intercession

The Purpose of Campmeetings for the Body of Christ

Books by Dr. Ben Campbell Johnson

The Heart of Paul

Matthew and Mark

For a complete list of books, video tapes, and
audio cassette tapes contact:

A Great Love, Inc.
P.O. Box 1248
Toccoa, Georgia 30577
(706) 886-5161